AUTHOR	CLASS
BARKER, A.L.	**F**

TITLE	No
Relative successes	484108985

RELATIVE SUCCESSES

Relative Successes

——

A. L. BARKER

CHATTO & WINDUS

THE HOGARTH PRESS

LONDON

Published in 1984 by
Chatto & Windus · The Hogarth Press
40 William IV Street
London WC2N 4DF

British Library Cataloguing in Publication Data

Barker, A. L. (Audrey Lilian)
Relative successes.
I. Title
823'.914[F]   PR6052.A647

ISBN 0-7011-2839-9

Photoset in Linotron Ehrhardt by
Rowland Phototypesetting Ltd
Bury St Edmunds, Suffolk
Printed in Great Britain by
Redwood Burn Ltd
Trowbridge, Wiltshire

'Success is relative: It is what we can make of the mess we have made of things.'

T. S. Eliot, *The Family Reunion*

I

Jessel was having difficulty with the new girl's name. It reminded him of the madwoman's attendant in *Jane Eyre*. It was absurd to think of this child with a matron's status. Mrs Poole indeed. When she came to clear his desk he held up his hand. 'Leave everything. I am staying a while longer.'

There was no point in telling her that he went out to supper on the first Thursday of every month and was accustomed, on those days, to working until six-thirty. He felt it would confuse her still further to try keeping track of his marginally business routines. A degree of confusion was necessary, even desirable: elasticity implied willingness to learn. At least she was not one of the young people who believed there was nothing worth learning.

'Leave the intercom switched through.'

He had seen, and regretted, the colour that rushed up from her neck when she was at a loss, and when she was trying, and succeeding. He would like to have assured her that it was superfluous, there was so much she could not be expected to know.

There was however great expectation in the room itself. The room conformed to senior executive standards, he was undeniably senior in years and did, to the best of his intention and belief, still execute on occasion. But looking up sometimes from unproductive thought he was aware of a constraint, a tongued and grooved disapproval. The office and its furnishings were intended for a well-fleshed, rosy-fingered, hard-nosed breed of men.

Don't worry, he had said to the girl, meaning that she should not worry on account of the lime panelling, the sculpted carpet and the king-sized desk. These were but the perfect attributes of an imperfect system. She had chosen to think he was rebuking her for her failure to produce the right files for the Chairman's meeting, she had cried 'I didn't know I had to put in for them in advance,' blaming herself whole-heartedly for her lack of knowledge. She was ginger-haired and freckled, a girl whom blushes did not become. 'I thought they'd be here, in the cabinet, I didn't know!' The strong pink with the old-fashioned ginger was all wrong. Jessel wondered at Nature's making such an error of judgment. When she cried dolefully, 'I ought to of asked!' he was quite disproportionately sorry for her.

He sat at his desk waiting for her to go. She made scrabbling noises in the outer office. Screwing up paper? Spoiled typesheets? Searching for something? Finishing her lunch? He went to the door and pulled it sharply open. She was struggling into long white boots with a cowboy fringe at the knee. 'Goodnight, Mrs Poole.'

Soon afterwards she went. He heard the door of the outer office close and there was silence. He supposed he would get used to her, and she to him. Her habituation, in the purely general sense, was important. What was not important, was scarcely necessary, was for her to adjust to his particular methods and foibles, for if her career with the Corporation was beginning, his was about to end.

That thought, which was never far from his mind, made him restive. He paced about, tapping his pockets, passing and re-passing the hospitality cupboard. Eventually he opened it. A drink would resolve nothing, least of all the prospect of his retirement, which he sometimes envisaged as being huge, scrupulous and devastating as a typhoon. Though entirely unspectacular. If, in most other respects it did resemble a typhoon and should be regarded as a natural calamity, he supposed the best thing to do was to keep his head down and wait for it to be over. It was what he proposed to do. The whisky encouraged him to think he had made up his mind.

He dictated two letters to the machine and a report on a small enterprise which, given the word, his Corporation might engorge. The word, in the position of trust he had now reached, was for him to give. At six-thirty he pushed everything into a drawer and put on his coat. He left always at the same time, giving himself half an hour to get to Bismarck Road. Miss Ranmore, his previous secretary, had called it his Bismarck night. He smiled as a tribute to her. They had sustained a perfect working relationship. It occurred to him that Miss Ranmore must have seen to that. She had seen the sort of man he was and subjugated her own tendencies. He thought that she might have had tendencies. She was a graduate of one of the old commercial schools which taught that a good secretary respects and defers to the temperament of her employer. Without his knowing more than he wished to know about her, and with her knowing only what he saw fit to tell her and what she might gather or infer about himself, they had worked together for many years. At her retirement party she had spoken of those times as some of the happiest of her life. Jessel, for whom they had not been wholly good or wholly happy years, was alarmed. But of course the badness and unhappiness had been his own affairs entirely: why should he expect – he certainly had no wish – that Miss Ranmore should see into his heart? Mrs Poole, he sighed, Mrs Poole was an infant.

While washing his hands he looked in the mirror. It was lonely at this time, between the departure of staff and the arrival of the cleaners. This was probably the loneliest place in the building; he thought it had something to do with the reflective surfaces. A pair of taps winkled him out, exposed and multiplied him. The mirrors multiplied the emptiness. There was a quite passable demonstration of infinity in the men's washroom.

His face was tiresomely familiar and hid nothing. He hoped that other people, though tired of it, might be uninformed enough to miss a few clues; the likenesses to his father, for instance, and his mother. The older he got, the more indissolubly he saw them in himself. He would have said it was impossible for those two to merge, yet there they were, his father's tapering cranium and his mother's blunt, homely muzzle. And something else: the played-out anarchy there had been between them. It showed in him as self-deprecation which he acknowledged in the way his mouth closed after speech.

He invariably reached Bismarck Road at seven, give or take a minute or two. He had formed the habit, while he was serving on a committee which met on the first Thursday of each month in a hall at one end of the road, of dropping in on his friends, the Kleins, at the other end. The committee had long since disbanded, but it was an understood thing that on the first Thursday of the month he went to the Kleins. He understood it. They took his coming, his continuing to come, for granted.

The upper end of Bismarck Road opened out with some public buildings, a church, the hall where his committee used to meet, and the local magistrates' court. The Kleins lived in a terrace house at the other, private, end. It was a Victorian house, the medium-rare brickwork, coloured tiles and pagoda-boarding were not congruous. Jessel was fond of it. As he pushed open the gate which carried an enamel plaque with the words, 'No Hawkers, No Canvassers, No Circulars', he smiled his appreciation. The Kleins, he could be reasonably sure, saw no discrepancies.

Connie, his wife, on the only occasion he had taken her to visit them, had laughed all the way home. He had been dismayed on her account, for it showed what a loss she was at and how unprincipled she could be. In trying to laugh at the Kleins – it was essentially a try – she had given herself away. Yet again. It was no longer a revelation by which he might help her, and himself. It had become an irreversible default. 'That place!' She had panicked, turned on him in defiance. 'It's a hoot, an absolute hoot. Surely you can see it? How can you *not*?' He had reminded her, 'It's only a house,' and she had cried, 'It's *their* house, that's how, that's why you can't see anything funny about it.' He had asked was anything else a hoot, careful not to isolate the word or apportion it to her, were they, the Kleins? She had said, 'No, that's the point, isn't it?'

Afraid, and taking character for comedy, she had snatched at it. That was the point. He peered through the stained glass panels of the Kleins' front door. Through an amber triangle he saw a hand. The fingers, dipping to the latch, turned ruby red.

Waldo's wife opened the door and said 'Jess,' non-interrogatively

[4]

and without inflection, as she always did. Jessel kissed her cheek. The kiss, too, was an invariable procedure and might have been taken by Connie as an act of fondness on his part, an intimacy which she did not share. It could have been why she had seized on laughter to maintain herself.

The bead curtain spanning the hall made a beetle-like clicking as they went through. That was another invariable and was one of the things Connie had chosen to laugh at. 'It's always been there,' he had said, 'it was there when they took over the house.' 'They didn't have to leave it there!' 'They like it, Waldo says it reminds him of an old film with Dr Fu Manchu and Anna* May Wong.' 'What does it remind *her* of?' Connie's not being able to give Daisy her name, rather than the tone, which was deliberately sprightly, told him how profound was her feeling. He had tried to get to the source of it. 'Why don't you like them?' 'Have I said I don't? Have I ever said a word against them?' Wanting to isolate whatever it was, whatever she imagined, he had asked 'What is there to dislike?' She had cried, 'Absolutely nothing!' and given him the bright parrying smile she had kept from her youth.

Daisy went through to a room at the back and Jessel followed. It was their custom to have a drink while they waited for Waldo. Jessel picked up the bottle. He then fancied that the glass he was about to use had already been used. He sniffed it. Definitely it smelt of whisky.

Daisy, a small woman, folded herself into the depths of an armchair, sat on her feet and tucked her hands into her armpits. She looked compact.

Jessel put the used glass aside and took two clean ones. She was watching him. At least, her eyes followed his movements, but when he carried the drink to her she did not take it. She gazed up at him as if they were having a not very satisfactory conversation. Then she shook her head and shrugged, and Jessel, who had been going to ask was anything wrong, said 'What a day!', referring to the rain. He had already remarked on it when she opened the door to him, he had turned to check that his wet umbrella was securely propped in a corner of the porch and exclaimed, 'What a day!'

When he had seen Daisy for the very first time he had been disappointed on Waldo's account. No one, he would have said, was going to look twice at her. It was not apparent to him why Waldo had. But that was while he was still borrowing other people's standards where he had formed none of his own. Of women, at that time, his knowledge had been second-hand.

'How are you?' he asked her.

Many people did in fact look twice, when a fractional glance would have been in order and would certainly have sufficed. They could not be looking because of her beauty, she had big features, eyes set deep in the bone, a fleshy nose, long loose lips. Generality had been left out of her face and the impression she gave was of a very private nature.

Jessel always sat in the same chair, and in the same attitude, legs extended, ankles crossed, his back tucked into the back of the chair. Since Daisy never moved the furniture around he might by now have made his own mark on the carpet with the pressure of his heels. It would not worry Daisy if he had, and it would please him to leave a small domestic pledge of his presence.

'The rain has never ceased. Yesterday was the same. It started on Tuesday night.' He almost added, 'At ten minutes past ten.' One of the first drops had landed on the back of his hand. He had gone into the garden to examine the gap where his neighbour had cut down a hedge and had seen, as he could not while the hedge was there, the illuminated face of the Town Hall clock. He had experienced a sense of loss which he was being increasingly made aware of. He felt that he was losing on all sides, and now, a hedge.

Waldo would have laughed had he known. So far as Jessel was concerned he had laughed and known, he didn't miss much because Jessel had got into the habit of looking at things on his behalf, whether they were Waldo's things or not. It had begun years ago, as a safety measure, at the start of their association.

[6]

'How's Connie?' said Daisy.

'Connie's very well.'

'What does she do while you're here?' He looked at her in surprise. 'You don't know, do you? Can't you make something up?'

He said stiffly, 'She doesn't mind.'

'Mind what?'

'Being on her own.'

'Lucky old Connie.' Daisy's hands were still tucked into her armpits. Waldo said she sat like a two-bladed knife. 'Lucky old you.'

He didn't know her all that well. As Waldo's wife it hadn't been necessary, it had hardly been possible. 'Waldo's late.'

'Would you like to eat?'

'No, we'll wait. I wonder what's keeping him. The rain, probably.' She did something with her mouth, pushed out her lower lip and shut down the top one. It wasn't a smile, but left him no choice to take it as anything else. 'It's more difficult to get a bus when it's wet.'

'You don't have that problem.'

It was voiced as a statement, a reminder to herself, without rancour, that he had a company car.

'Where to park can be a problem. Tonight I had to go into the church forecourt at the other end of the road.' He could guess what Waldo saw in her, and could envy him for seeing it. He himself would have passed it by, looking for something else.

'This is the sukebind position.' Daisy unlocked her arms and began unseating herself from her feet. It occurred to Jessel that she had been drinking. He remembered the used glass. 'Cold comfort.' She reached for the back of the chair, missed, and staggered.

He could not try to help for fear of embarrassing her by the implication. He said, when she was steady on her feet, 'I have a new secretary. Miss Ranmore has gone to Ireland to live with her widowed brother.'

'Pretty?'

'Oh no.'

'The new girl, I mean.' She stood on her toes, then sank on to her

[7]

heels, several times, as if to exercise her ankles. She was, he felt, obliging herself to think about his concerns.

'Neither she nor Miss Ranmore could claim to be that.'

'Shame.' She smiled and, her obligation ended, went into the kitchen. He heard her clattering saucepans, through the open door saw her putting her inconsiderable hips about with a kind of vengeful energy.

He had no wish to know what was wrong, it was not incumbent on him to know and he felt resentment at there being wrong. The fault, or error, misconception, misconstruction, whatever it was, would be attributable to her, for whatever was or went wrong with Waldo had always defied his definition. He called out, feeling that it was incumbent on him to bridge the pause, to keep her company, 'When I have had a personable secretary it has been a strain on us both. Everyone behaves as if you have a hetairal relationship and you are obliged to pretend that you do. And whether you do or not, you have to put up with innuendoes.' One girl, a temp, employed during Miss Ranmore's vacation, had burst into tears at a meeting of sales executives, following a dig, and meaningful laughter, about the 'window-dressing' of executive offices, with special reference to incidental douceurs, and Jessel had been obliged to comfort her in front of them all. At his diffident touch on her shoulder she had cried out that she was not perks. He had said, with the whole meeting listening and smiling, that no one thought so, that it was only a joke, no one was impugning her moral fibre. Of course they did, and they were, and even more were they impugning his, not the lack, but the excess of it. 'Some of my colleagues regard it as a matter of status to have a pretty girl in the outer office. They consider looks more important than efficiency. Of course young men expect both. Personally, I prefer someone who has nothing extraneous to live up to, someone who will give her whole mind to her work. Conventional good looks are not necessarily an asset in business. First impressions are important, they may be the only ones people will have time to form, but too much perfection can be off-putting. A plain face in a handsome room is reassuring, people feel that ability is being given its chance, and they take it as proof of the sound sense of the company. They like to think that virtue does not have to be its own reward.' It was his own theory and he was developing it. 'One could cite our Managing Sales Director as an example. He is barely thirty and can afford to go to a royal duke's tailor, but he is a very homely-looking man.'

She called out, 'You're not.'

'Thank you.'

She appeared in the kitchen doorway. 'You're old, though.' He was hurt. He was trying not to think about it the way other people did, what he believed was the universally wrong way, based – or rather, skewed – on a few unavoidable truths. He was trying to get senescence into perspective. She leaned her head against the door jamb. 'Awfully old.'

It ceased to hurt. He suspected that to her, just then, the world and everything in it was old. He had never seen her look so tired.

'A patriarchal appearance also helps the representation.' He avoided using the word 'image' which, if right, was too right: it conveyed an illusion existing only in the mind's eye. Perhaps she was deliberately overdoing the weariness. Connie sometimes did: pretending utter exhaustion seemed to reanimate her. But for Daisy there was another resource. 'Waldo says I made the most of being old even in school.' He expected the name to help her, but with a purely reflexive movement she rolled her shoulders across the door jamb, rolled herself round it and went back into the kitchen.

Actually, Waldo had caused him to feel shamefully young when he was at school, and only later, at an unspecified but opportune moment, had taken to making him feel irremediably old. Jessel raised his voice.

'Perhaps I should write a confidential memo to our personnel department on the desirability of a lack of looks and a sufficiency of years in whoever takes over my job when I retire.'

'Why not?'

'Of course I'm only joking. Personal recommendations are not encouraged. Our Corporation is, if anything, too democratic – boards and committees and quorums, there's too much representation and not enough direct influence. That is my opinion for what it is worth.' He smiled his downturned smile. 'In fact, my opinion is worth nothing. Advice, whether privileged information or the experience of a lifetime, is not welcome. I would go so far as to say it is suspect.' That was perhaps going too far and might give the impression of lack of trust. 'On the other hand, there is no nepotism. A corporation of such a size and importance could never come under individual management. And a ring, however well-motivated, would virtually control the life of the country. There are safeguards, of course. There is a ring of unions, not particularly well-motivated, but their interests are variously supplied. It is a matter of policy to keep them non-mutual –'

'Scrambled,' said Daisy, coming from the kitchen. 'All right with you?' She brought two plates. On each was a slice of toast and a mound of yellow egg. There were no knives and forks on the table, no condiments, no mats, no wine, no napkins. Not even a table-cloth. On the white dinner-plates the toast had slipped to one side, was threatening to slip right off. To straighten it would have looked like criticism.

'If they weren't, they could destroy us.'

'They?'

'The unions.'

'If they weren't what?'

'If they made common cause.'

She went to the sideboard, to fetch cutlery he thought. Instead, she filled the used glass he had seen earlier and brought it to the table. 'Let's eat.'

'Shan't we wait for Waldo?'

'No.'

She sat down and without ceremony took up the toast and bit into the bread and egg. It shocked him. People ought not to hand food into their mouths when there was an opportunity to use a knife and fork. Certainly not people he knew, certainly not Daisy Klein. What would Waldo say? It would be something jocular, to put her lapse into context. What context? Perhaps it was a likely lapse, one she was prone to in moments of abstraction. Was she abstracted? Thinking of something else? Her movements were decisive and almost violent. He had never been alone with her for long.

'Ah well, fingers came before thumbs,' he said. It gave away the fact that he had already observed the absence of cutlery. It would have come better as a humorous acceptance when he had actually sat down at the table, confronting his plate. 'How late will Waldo be?'

'You mean forks, don't you?' She drained her glass, held it before her face and looked at him through it.

She was not being playful; one of her eyes, magnified, stared unwinkingly. It was going to be a question of adjustment, taking her on her terms and not Waldo's. He hoped she would soon let him know what her terms were.

When he picked up his toast the egg, which was dry, fell off. He tried scooping it back, while she watched. She was definitely not abstracted, though he could not tell, from the magnified eye, what she was thinking. 'I worked late myself, or rather later, tonight. I always do when I'm coming here.'

'Why?'

'I wouldn't wish to arrive too early and get under your feet.'

'You can arrive when you like. Any time up to midnight. Any midnight.'

'I was thinking of the meal. Of you – preparing it.' Usually she took a lot more trouble, but he couldn't very well point that out. She was a good cook and there was always wine with the food, and the table set, and he had his own napkin ring. 'I wouldn't mind waiting.'

'What for?'

'For Waldo.'

'Oh yes you would.'

He had not yet touched the egg, he sat chafing his fingers in anticipation, aware that she was waiting to see that he picked it up. 'You need not have bothered solely on my account.'

She set her glass down with a bang. 'I'd forgotten you were coming.'

A chill went through him, he had immediate realisation of what the words meant in plain terms. Then panic gave way to unsurprise. He refused to be humiliated in her sight, whether or not she intended it. 'If I'd known it was inconvenient I wouldn't have come.'

'It's not a question of convenience. For me convenience is whether I take a bath or wash my hair or go to the launderette and your coming hasn't coincided with any of that.' He realised that she was in the process of snubbing him and must be allowed her say. He waited, but was unprepared for the crispness with which she said 'Waldo's gone.'

'Gone?'

'For good. Good for him. And for me.'

'Gone where?'

'Evidently he also forgot you were coming.'

'This is the first Thursday of the month. He knows I always come on the first Thursday of the month.'

'I hate scrambled egg, so why did I make it?' He felt that other things, besides eggs, were being scrambled. She leaned forward, a crumb on her lip. 'I made it for you.'

'Thank you. I like scrambled egg, I often have it for breakfast.'

'You can stay the night.'

'The night?'

'And eat your egg in the morning.' He had never known her without Waldo and had not succeeded in getting to know her with him. In his ignorance all he could do was examine her face and note how little space there was in it. 'Why not?' she said. 'We'll be quite alone.'

'Thank you, but I'm expected home. I'm sorry about the egg. I had a business lunch, rather heavy, finishing with rhubarb crumble – something I'm partial to. So you see I'm not really hungry.'

'You might be in the morning.' She got up and replenished her glass.

He understood that he must give her the benefit of the doubt, he shouldn't even be doubting, he had never done so before. Without being positive about anything about her – except that she was Waldo's wife, because she was Waldo's wife – he had not questioned what she said or did. 'Where is Waldo?'

'I don't know.'

'Are you telling me that Waldo – that you and Waldo –'

'It isn't me and Waldo, it's just me.'

Her features had darkened. Her lips, thin-skinned and the colour of mulberry, were softly bunched and tremulous where a moment ago they were square and hard, her tongue forked out and the words came off it flecked with spittle. She had always aroused a degree of ambivalent feeling in him, to a quite small degree attracted and repelled him.

'What happened?' Without her, Waldo would not be less than himself: what he lacked and she supplied was fairly generally obtainable. Jessel said, 'I thought you were happy.' He had told Connie, 'They're happy,' and she had said, 'Is that what they are?' He had been angry, but not with her. A cold anger turned round and round like a dog settling, and it had settled in his stomach and griped for days. Connie was, and always had been, mishandled, and he knew where to put the blame for that. 'Tell me what happened.'

'I'm not telling anyone.' She went again to the sideboard and brought the bottle to the table. He locked his hands and held them between his knees. He wanted an answer and she had it, and with a fraction more anger, or less control, he would shake it out of her. 'Own up,' she said, 'you're glad he's gone. It's what you've been waiting for.' He promptly suspended all feeling as the only way of dealing with what looked alarmingly like a developing situation. When she said, 'There's just me now. Isn't that what you want?' he allowed the words but not what they might signify.

'I could talk to Waldo if I knew where he was. Surely it's only a temporary disagreement?' He did not bat an eyelid. 'We all have our differences, sometimes they seem irreconcilable. But a little talk, a discussion in cooler blood, a little give and take, and they can be resolved. I might be able to help, act as an intermediary. It's the least I can do.'

'It's the most.' She took the bottle up by its neck. 'You're no earthly fun.'

II

The conclusion that Jessel's housemaster had come to was that Jessel was an impeded personality. At every school there were boys who could not mix and parents were justifiably alarmed at the implications. As there was nothing parents could do – it had been their doing, anyway, in the first place – unmiscibility was not mentioned in end of term reports. Jessel had been advised to try to join in. He rather overdid it: a memory which his school-fellows might have cherished for its grotesqueness was the vision of him beating about the football field like a demented stork.

His housemaster supposed that what impeded him was a wrong upbringing. But Jessel had not been brought up, he had been left to make his own way. His father and mother were mutually self-sufficing. They found in each other a microcosm of the whole of life; love and hate, peace and war, parent and child. They had had no wish for a bona fide infant. Jessel was an unwarrantable intrusion. They packed him off first with nurses and then to school. He was not an engaging child and too reticent to become a button-holing one. There had been a succession of nurses during his formative years. He learned how pointless it was to rely on anyone, least of all himself, and tried to provide for his own protection by anticipating his shortcomings. He was careful not to impinge, he concealed and curtailed his reactions and withstood all approaches. His attempts to mix were really attempts to merge. He had thought he was succeeding and was dismayed when Waldo Klein singled him out with an invitation for the holidays.

Waldo neither mixed nor merged. He outclassed by his non-conformity. There was no question of his being better than anyone else, standards didn't apply. Jessel loved and envied Waldo's independence, but there had to be limits. He waited, as a matter of common justice, for Waldo to come a cropper and it looked as if he was putting his foot wrong when he sought Jessel as a companion. He must know that Jessel did not come up to general expectations and Waldo's were sure to be specific.

'I'm afraid I can't,' said Jessel. 'I have things to do.'

'What things?'

'Engagements. Et cetera.'

'Engagements who with?'

'People.'

'What people?'

'Friends.' Jessel added, with his downturned smile, 'And ene-mies.' Actually he had nothing to do and no one to see. People would see him, see that he was present, and that was all. He would be required to keep his voice down and be on time for meals. The only individual act that would be expected of him would be that he return to school on the day the holidays ended.

'We've got horses,' said Waldo.

'I can't ride.'

'I'll teach you.'

'I don't think!'

'It's easy. You grip the belly with your knees and when the horse goes up you go up and when it comes down you come down. If you're coming down when it's coming up you get a sore arse.'

Jessel looked into Waldo's face. If he had been born free, how had he? By what accident? Whose design? Jessel knew about genes and had a rough idea how they worked. It looked like luck. So where was common justice?

'We go to the Med. Same place every year. Swimming, sailing, and I can get hold of a car. Drive you into Italy.' Jessel nodded, stiff-necked. 'We can do what we like. No one lifts a finger. My mother doesn't and there's just her and me. She's a raving beauty, my mother.'

Something hot and emulsifying spread up from Jessel's stomach and down to his knees. He understood that he was being tempted. And in the end he went, not for the horses or the boat or the laissez-faire or the ravishing Mrs Klein, but because someone had tried to tempt him.

In the train to Dover he asked, 'Why me? Why not Forbes? Or Plumley? Or Phipps? They're your friends.' He meant to have it clear from the outset, purely as a safety measure, that he was not presuming.

'It's a notion I have.'

'What notion?'

Waldo put his feet up on the seat, linked his hands behind his head and shut his eyes. 'I have it, that's all.'

Jessel, who had been unable to prevent himself hoping that Waldo might say, 'I asked because I like you,' had already dismissed the hope as flummery. He had been given to understand that he was not likeable and he understood it. There was nothing in him to like, judging by what was liked in other people. In those days, although he was aware of his inadequacy, he had no idea what it amounted to. Obviously there was something he was going to have to do without – without letting anyone see that he was without it.

Waldo went to sleep and Jessel was able to spend some time watching his face. There was nothing else to watch, the train was running through Kentish towns of slate roofs and coal-bunkers. It was then, without invitation, that Waldo began to get under Jessel's skin. Jessel particularly wanted to keep what there was of himself to himself and Waldo Klein was the last person he would have chosen to admit to his private thought processes. He was pretty sure that Waldo was uninterested in them as a matter of principle, infiltration would have taken planning and intent. This was more like a contagion which he, Jessel, would be exposed to for the whole of the holiday. He almost got out at the next station.

At the next station Waldo opened his eyes. 'Forbes is a rotten liar.'

'What?'

'He's rotten at lying. Can't con anyone.'

'You want someone conned?'

'Plumley runs after women and Phipps has hay-fever. I don't want Plumley running after my mother.' Jessel understood – Plumley had a wet dropsical mouth and smelt of dog – and was slightly encouraged. 'Of course running might come into the action. Just simple legging.'

'What action?'

'Any action. I expect some. Don't you?'

Jessel looked out of the window and saw through the open door of a privy a broad wooden seat and a telephone directory hanging on a string. He was not to forget, the train flashing past fixed it in his mind's eye. To him it was a snap judgment, delivered by a source that was setting him up, the inference being that what he would do, the sort of thing he could be relied on to do, would turn out squalid, comic, and of the lowest human denomination.

'Do you drive?' said Waldo.

'No.'

'Have you got brothers and sisters?'

'No.'

'Do your parents live together?'

'Yes.'

'My mother left my father before I was born. Mind you, they weren't married. He was twenty years older than her.'

Jessel, feeling his face blanch, said, 'So you're a bastard?'

Waldo swung his feet to the floor, sat up and asked did he mind.

Jessel said, 'Not me. I don't give a damn, but my parents will.'

'Are they terribly strict?'

'They're terribly particular.'

'Keep you wrapped in cotton wool?'

'That's what they'd like to think.'

'They don't have to know everything.'

'I'm supposed to tell them everything.'

'And do you?'

'Naturally not. My father keeps a record of all my friends, what their parents are, where they live, what sort of house, how many bathrooms, how many servants, how much ground they've got.' He found he was quite a serviceable liar. 'All the relevant background information.'

'What does he do?'

'Do?'

'What's his line of business, how does he make his dough?'

Jessel said the first thing that came into his head. 'He's a High Court Judge.'

'Cheee.' Waldo whistled. 'Well, here's what he can record about me. Only son of an impoverished but high-born widow, family mansion in Shropshire, villa in South of France, twenty rooms in a hundred acres, household staff of ten, a string of horses, a sea-going yacht.'

'Is it true?'

'True enough. My mother was born in the Alps. That's high.' Waldo knocked down a finger at a time as he enumerated each point. 'Family mansion – no need to say whose family. Villa has plenty of rooms, though there's no ceiling in some of them. A hundred acres of ground – why not? There's ground all round.'

'It's wilful misrepresentation.'

'So?'

'My father would give you six years.' Jessel, whose father was a sanitary engineer, found that he was enjoying himself.

'Is he a hanging judge?'

'Naturally. He cries like a baby after he's put on the black cap.'

Waldo said, 'He must be a bit of a bastard himself.'

'He tends to concentrate on me. He wants me to do all the things he hasn't been able to.'

'How much scope does that leave you?'

'All the right things,' Jessel said firmly. 'My parents want me to have the best.' At the beginning of the holidays his mother had looked at him with a flicker of curiosity. 'You're growing up.' The thought did not persist long enough to please or annoy her. She had turned away, letting it evaporate.

Waldo swung his feet back on the seat and pillowed his head on his arms. 'You could tell him I'm related to the Waldorf Kleins of New York.'

The woman Jessel had no choice but to call Mrs Klein turned out to be thoroughly pretty. Jessel was thorough in his appreciation. He did not recognise the signs and accepted in all innocence that the fine scarlet threads below the surface of her skin were what gave it its rose tint. He did not doubt that the heart-stopping contrast between her golden hair and her black eyelashes was ordered by Nature. It did indeed stop his heart, and re-started it with a lumpy motion. She had plump hands and a voluptuous bosom which she presented in low-cut dresses on a bed of lace. Jessel, never much of a voluptuary, found himself speculating on circumferences, weight and displacement areas, aware at the same time that it was something he should not be doing.

Waldo called her pet names: Bunny, Mouse, Skeeter, Baba, though she was patently neither a rabbit nor a mouse nor a mosquito nor an infant. She was more of a cat. That, Jessel decided, was due to her softness and the warmth from her skin and her winking stare and the way she stretched herself, opening and closing her fingers and, as he saw when she went barefoot, her toes. When she poured coffee or shut a window or unfolded a newspaper she did so with an economy of movement which was itself a grace. And an intimacy. She was kind, occasionally she touched Jessel lightly and inquiringly with her finger. His skin stood up in mountains.

The villa was a farm, La Bigorne, owned by people called Crau, and the farmhouse was built over the barn and stables. Bits of straw were constantly coming up through the floorboards. Goats, hens, oxen and a mule occupied the stables. Jessel asked about the car and Waldo pointed to some oil stains on the floor of the barn and said it had gone to be repaired. His mother did not own the place, she and Waldo were paying guests. Jessel supposed she was paying for him and fretted about how to get the money from his parents. Waldo said they were en famille and nobody could charge for a room without a ceiling.

Jessel was unable to identify the members of the Crau family, even in their context of the farm. He never saw them working. They spoke, or rather exploded, a patois which his school French could not fathom. They were dark-complexioned, with overhung foreheads and brilliant apeish eyes. The women dressed in rusty black, the men in singlets and bright blue trousers. Waldo said their clothes were stained with the stuff they sprayed on the vines. They crackled with life in its more basic forms, seemed not so much to be feeling as demonstrating what could be felt, and how. Their ebullience unnerved Jessel. They shouted, raged and openly wept – the men as well as the women – and next minute screamed with laughter. The children either took a dislike or a fancy to him for they followed him about, a dozen at a time, keeping their distance, staring long and silently, and at an ungiven moment and for no discernible reason were all convulsed with laughter and ran away, choking en masse.

'How many of them are there?'

'I told you,' said Waldo, 'everything's en famille. You know what that means?'

'Of course.'

'It means incest.'

'What?'

'This is a backward place. The men take their pick of the women and the women call the kids after the saints, to put matters right.'

Jessel had gone cold and then hot. Waldo was always copping him like that, frightening him stiff and then causing him to boil with feelings which he didn't know he had.

Jessel's room had a ceiling, cracked like the shell of a well-tapped egg. There was a complex smell of what he called to himself 'ancience'. It was even in the sheets of his bed – especially in his bed – and added another dimension. He found he was referring to it when he was not actually in the house, he was coming to rely on the smells of old timber and plaster and dust slung in cobwebs. He believed he could smell the long hot summers before this one. He was not a sensualist but he could, on occasion, relish the evidence of one of his senses. The yacht turned out to be a dinghy which didn't belong to Waldo or to the Craus. It was beached on the rocks of a little bay miles from the farm. If they went early enough Waldo and Jessel could launch it before the owner arrived to stop them. There were no horses on the farm. There wasn't a bathroom, not one, just a basin and ewer in his bedroom.

He could appreciate, and be glad, that there were no fixed battlegrounds either. At home certain areas had histories of encounters and skirmishes and he moved in them as gingerly and as aware as if they had been wired off. At home he constantly heard the sounds of battle, past, present and future. They were probably enjoyed, but not by him.

The people at La Bigorne were alien, their raised voices merely signified another hot day, along with the crowing cocks and whirring crickets. And there was no espionage. The children watched him openly and without prospect. As their curiosity dwindled, so did they. Finally only one child retained sufficient interest to gaze and giggle at him.

At La Bigorne one thing might lead to another, or simply fall apart. Jessel, conditioned to seeing his parents lock events together to make war, was bothered at first by the wasted opportunities. It seemed reprehensible when he thought how they would have been seized upon and used at home. He had always believed that his parents' way was the only way to live and that he must either learn it or accustom himself to a partial existence. He had wondered why Waldo should be so lucky and if he owned his luck or if it was temporary and would go away. He had thought that even if it did, the good would have been done, for Waldo could never find himself in anything like Jessel's situation.

Waldo and his mother did not fight. It was impossible to envisage Mrs Klein in a rage or in any extreme of emotion. Hers was the ideally adjusted state and gave her the better of everything. To Jessel it was the ideal to be striven for. She, of course, did not have to strive. She was a prototype, he accepted that as a scientific fact. And that Waldo had inherited it from her. Waldo's freedom was a straight genetical connection and common justice was nowhere.

At La Bigorne he came close to being happy. He assumed that what he felt was happiness. It was really a sort of exemption, a non-liability, no sooner recognised than gone. Of course there was a strong element of idiocy in happiness, but some people could handle it and manage to avoid making fools of themselves. They took it in their stride, as Waldo did. Added to everything else that Waldo had, and was, happiness must matter less to him than it did to Jessel.

Waldo required reactions and at school could count on getting them. At La Bigorne he had provided Jessel. In the mornings he went to Jessel's room and kicked the leg of his bed to wake him. Once it was four a.m., he wanted to go fishing and they had a long ride to the bay.

The sea looked awful that day, so did the sky, dirty and creeping. The sea crept out to the horizon and great bagging clouds crept in. A yellowish scurf was spreading over the rocks. Jessel thought he had never seen anything so vile. Of course it wasn't the time to be seeing anything.

'Let's go back to bed,' he said, to register his protest, to let it be known that he didn't want to be there. Waldo, hauling in the boat, shouted back something about the sirocco and flung the end of a sopping wet rope. It hit Jessel in the face, like a poke from the elements. The elements were on the loose, ready to rampage, he could feel their violence through the soles of his feet. He felt that it was cocked and ready in the sand.

'Heave!' Waldo lay back along the rope. 'One, two, three baby-oh!' The prow of the boat hit a deep-water shelf and rebounded. 'Get aboard!'

'No thanks, I'll get my feet wet.'

The next moment Waldo had seized him by the knees and hoisted him in his arms like a big child. He waded out, carrying Jessel, and dropped him over the side of the boat. Jessel's feet went straight into a pool of black water.

'This thing's sinking!'

'Always does,' Waldo said blithely. 'Takes about four hours to go down and we'll be back before then.'

'I'd rather not risk it.'

Waldo shoved an oar at him. 'Pull away.'

'I can't row.'

'Watch me and you'll learn.' He was a powerful oarsman. Also the sea sucked them out. Jessel saw with alarm how fast the shore receded. He lifted his feet clear of the water – the bilge, he supposed – and the wind cut between his legs. He worried that he might get piles, but that was probably the least that would happen to him. 'Bait the hooks,' said Waldo.

'What?'

'They're right behind you. Stick a bit of the grub in the bucket on each one.'

Jessel received another blast of chilly air up his trousers. He put the bucket between his knees, accepting without stoicism that worse could come. It came when his fingers, reaching into the bucket, touched and were obliged to retain an unspeakable grey ball. 'What's this?'

'What's it look like?'

'The reproductive organs of small mammals.'

Waldo shouted with laughter. 'Cut it in half or the fish will grab it off the hook.'

Jessel made up his mind not to eat anything Waldo caught because it would have eaten the bait. Then the sea began to tip them about and he knew he would not be eating again anyway. He sat pressing a hook into his stomach to keep his guts still. A squall of rain which he could see coming in rods out of a specific cloud arrived overhead and emptied into the boat.

'Start bailing,' said Waldo.

'If we go back I will.'

'We shan't get back if you don't.'

Waldo stood in the prow, his wet trousers clapped round his thighs. He landed small fish, all fins and tails, and then a big black thing with teeth.

'God, what is it?'

'A tiger shark.'

'Get away!'

'A young one, about three months old. They take years to get to full size, you know.'

'Sharks? In these waters?'

'Why not? The Pacific's overfished and they're being forced out. They come here to breed.'

'There's no way they could, except over ground. Do you suggest they walk it?'

'They jump up the rivers, like trout.' Waldo dragged the fish into the bottom of the boat. 'As a matter of fact it's been proved that under the earth, if you go down far enough, all the seas run into each other.'

Jessel was reasonably sure that it was another demonstration of the way Waldo put things together for his own amusement. 'Aren't you going to kill it?'

'Of course not.' The fish was leaping up and down, snapping the air with its jaws. Jessel swivelled sideways, holding his feet out of its reach. Waldo said, 'I only kill when necessary.'

'I don't like mess.'

'There won't be any.'

'How will you kill it?'

'Knock it on the head.'

'Do it then.'

'Not yet. It's for tomorrow's supper and we haven't an ice-box.' Waldo sank on his haunches in the prow and looked at Jessel. 'There's a time for killing.'

The fish, jumping and falling, jumping and falling into the dirty water at the bottom of the boat somehow affronted Jessel's self-respect. He threw the bait overboard and clapped the bait bucket over the fish.

'Why did you do that?'

'Because I don't want to see it.'

'I had to buy that bait, fishing's an expensive business.'

'I'll pay.'

Waldo held out his hand. 'Two-fifty.'

Jessel gave him a franc. 'If you paid more than that you were done.'

Waldo grinned and pocketed the money. Jessel was reasonably sure that he had not paid a centime for the stuff in the bucket.

Mrs Klein was walking on the hillside above the farm when they got back. She moved with a bated motion and Jessel, constrained as usual to observe her, saw how she paused every now and then. Waldo left his bicycle lying in the farm gateway and cut across the yard to her. Jessel propped his machine up against the wall. It was apparent and, to him, memorable, how she stirred one foot from the other to advance a few paces. He was shocked when he saw that she was barefoot. She appeared to be deliberating with her toes. He watched them delicately splayed and then curling and gripping the grass.

She looked up. 'I couldn't sleep,' and added, more to herself than to him, 'Elderly ladies often don't.'

He blurted, 'You're not elderly!' and saw by her smile that she would have expected as much from him, had she thought about it. 'Un vrai galant,' she said softly.

Poker stiff, he asked her pardon.

'Oh my dear, didn't you mean it?'

'Don't tease, Skeeter,' said Waldo.

She stretched out her hand, but did not actually touch Jessel. His skin stood up nonetheless. He observed that she had very little on. Her dress was cut even lower than usual and was of some terribly fine material that clothed her skin-tight when the wind blew, which it did all the time. Every crevice of her body was lined with silk. Jessel averted his eyes. The pink quilted coat she wore lifted behind her like wings, she floated, smiling and dreaming, her feet still greedily seeking the grass. It occurred to Jessel that she might be in her nightdress.

Startled, he turned to look again, and Waldo at that moment put an arm across his throat and started to throttle him. They fell, silently fighting. Jessel, the lighter weight and a non-combatant, was soon pinned face down, with Waldo astride him.

Waldo pushed his face into a tussock and held it there. Jessel was in some danger of suffocating. It was possible that he would suffocate, anything was possible with Waldo. What he saw, passing before him, was not his past life, but Mrs Klein, silken-skinned and plundering.

At a last moment, one of the very last it seemed to Jessel, Waldo rolled off him. Jessel sat up, gasping and sucking in air. He felt a fool, and in those days of youthful egotism his foolishness was universal. He believed that everyone knew of it and laughed. He looked first for Mrs Klein because her laughter mattered most.

She was a hundred yards away, levelling with a clump of pines. She had either seen enough, or seen nothing. He got to his feet as the first drops of rain arrived. A phalanx of water was approaching along the valley.

'They're going to get wet,' said Waldo.

'They?'

Waldo aimed his thumb. Jessel saw that someone was reaching up from the ground beneath the pines. He knew that it was a man, his clothes were the colour of the blue stuff they sprayed the vines with. Then Mrs Klein sank down, covering the blue with her tender pink.

'Who's that with her?'

'Louis or Babert or Rizzo or Gilles. Perhaps it's old Crau himself.'

'Don't you care?'

The rain drove into Waldo's wide open eyes but he did not blink. 'Shall we go and look?' Jessel's heart leaped into his mouth. He felt sick. 'You'd like to, wouldn't you?' Waldo said softly, as if he was proposing a treat.

Jessel turned and ran in the opposite direction, pitching and once falling to his knees. He wouldn't have liked to go and see, but he badly wanted to. It was the same compulsion as he might feel about seeing a gruesome accident.

By the time he got to the farmhouse he was soaked through. He delayed changing his clothes to stand at the window of his room looking across to the pines. The rain had blotted them out. He was thinking, of course, of Mrs Klein. It was awful how busy his thoughts were, though not with her so much as with the pink thing she had on. He thought about her below the neck because the pink thing didn't come any higher. He thought about it getting wet and dark, going deep into every hollow of her body and then swelling out again. There were places where it would swell like a balloon; there is nothing so shameless as a fully inflated balloon. He was surprised at how many details he was able to supply, details hitherto unsuspected and certainly unknown. Again and again he tried to turn his thoughts away, for as well as self- and more general disgust, there was the insult to Mrs Klein. His hostess. She would neither forget nor forgive, she would be irrevocably defiled. And there was Waldo, who knew his thoughts. Waldo had already expressed his views about Plumley, the runner after women.

All the time he was changing out of his wet clothes he was watching the window, watching for the pines to reappear. As suddenly as it had begun, the rain stopped. There was an instant curdling of the air, a rolling back, across the hills, right out to the horizon. The pines came up sharp and clear as if they had been cut out of tin. Jessel sighed, with a sense of gross insufficiency.

When he went down to the farm kitchen to look for something to eat Waldo was already there. So was one of the old women. There were many old women, Jessel knew because he had seen them together. To him they were interchangeable. They all wore black bell skirts, their thin legs coming out from underneath like clappers.

They all nodded and muttered and winked. There was an element of malice about them. It was contained in their burnt-out bodies and was impartial: it was feared, respected, even revered. The old women were served first at table, deferred to, listened to when they chose to speak out, and given a wide-ish berth. He had never seen anyone lay a finger on them, in anger or affection.

Waldo was drinking coffee out of a bowl. Jessel took a cup and filled it from the enamel pot on the stove. The farm bread was grey and sour-tasting. Waldo, who had dropped a crust into his bowl, fished out the sop and put it in his mouth. 'Like castor oil and water,' he said indistinctly, 'one helps the other down.'

'You'll eat snails next.'

'I have done. Fried in butter they're a revelation.'

'I'd like an egg. Je veux manger un oeuf.' Jessel addressed himself to the old woman who was stringing beans. 'Un oeuf bouilli, s'il vous plaît.'

Something awful happened. It was as if she had been split from brow to chin. Her face disappeared, sucked in or blown out. Jessel was looking at a black hole. He realised that she was laughing. She had no teeth and her eyes glittered from depths of bone.

'She swallows eggs whole,' said Waldo.

'Don't talk rot.'

'I tell you, it's her party piece. She'll do it for you if she likes you. You can actually see the egg going down her gullet. They bring the biggest one they can find and the men bet on whether she'll get it down without breaking the shell. She doesn't always. She tried a turkey's egg and nearly choked to death. They hit her on the windpipe to crack the shell and relieve the pressure.'

'She's evil.'

'I don't think she likes you.'

Jessel drank his coffee. It at least was good, and gave him a lift.

'She'll do it for me,' said Waldo. 'I don't have to ask. She just picks up an egg, puts it in her mouth and points to her throat. She's got a neck like a boa-constrictor's.'

The old woman had her face back and was using it to munch and wink. When Waldo spoke, she nodded her head with a kind of merciless tic.

Jessel turned his eyes away from her. 'If it's you she fancies, you're welcome.'

The pines were not visible from the kitchen. A tamarisk hedge interposed. Jessel stood looking into the yard. All there was to see were the movements of a hen, one hen, strategically quartering the mud. Enormous care seemed to have been taken in the disposition of the straws which floated across the puddles all in the same direction without arriving at the other side. The thick yellow air that couldn't hold a shadow was slotted into the fronds of the tamarisk so that he should think nothing was going on.

'I say,' Waldo called to him, 'remember that notion I had?'

'What notion?'

'About you.'

'How can I remember when I don't know what it was?'

'I still have it.'

Jessel, by then, was cottoning on to how to handle Waldo a little more for his own comfort. If he wanted repercussions the thing to remember was that Waldo wanted them more. If, as now, he didn't care either way, he had the advantage.

'You're close,' said Waldo, 'you don't go around blabbing. It isn't your style.' To be called close-mouthed was, on the whole, a compliment. Waldo must know that it was due more to incapability than discretion. Still, Jessel felt encouraged. 'And you're quite resourceful. A bit nervy, but I'll soon steady you up.'

'Will you?'

'The way I look at it,' said Waldo cheerfully, 'if you can't get everything in one packet you settle for the packet with the most. I reckon you've got the most for me.'

It wasn't exactly a declaration of friendship, there was something commercial about the way he pulled his nose as he spoke.

'Delighted, I'm sure.'

'I want you to help me with something.' Jessel made a non-committal face. 'It's big. It will be the biggest thing I've ever done.' Waldo eyed him soberly, 'I'm asking you because you're the only one I can trust.'

'Asking me what?'

'To help me kill my mother.'

There was a brief noisy recession, like the running back of the sea or the echo of a bell. Then Jessel, anxious more than shocked, did what was expected. For once it was easy. He laughed, which was patently the right thing to do. He said heartily, having unquestionably found his heart, 'Oh sure. Trust me for that.'

'Good.'

'You know what I thought you said?'

'Yes. That's what I said.'

To laugh was the right thing to do, to have done, then proceed to something else. Ridicule. Scorn. 'Go pawn your arse.'

'I'm open to fair comment.'

Indignation. Anger. 'Look here, what are you playing at? What do you take me for?' Jessel knew the answer to that. The justice of it eluded him, but justice there was. Somewhere along the line of this holiday it had been proved. 'I'm not a fool.' He raged at those powers into whose hands he was invariably delivered. 'Damn you!'

Waldo, at sixteen, had cheeks solid as apples. With his eyes wide and his jaw dropped he was positively homely. 'Why? What did I do?'

'You're not clever, you're not funny, you're filthy-minded, Klein. Nothing's too foul, you'd think anything, say anything!'

'What did I say?'

'I know your game –'

'What I said was I want you to help me kill my mother.' There was another pause, absolute silence this time. Jessel stood quiet as a lamb. Waldo crossed his arms on his breast. 'And that's it.'

His quietness began to grow on Jessel. It took root, spread, assumed enormous proportions. It was like the change in the weather, for all he knew there was no place or circumstance where it did not pertain.

'Why?' That was the next question, and whether it was right or not to ask, it was logical.

'I don't have to tell you that.'

'I should have thought I'm the one you've got to tell.'

'You know already.'

'Go to blazes.'

Jessel should have gone, walked out and kicked a ball around or taken the bus, anything to show detachment. He should be completely disassociated, not willing nor able to be pulled into any mad, bad and unfunny caper Waldo Klein was purposing. But he did not have the right attitude. He felt only conspiracy and occlusion and the old suspicion that he was being singled out.

'Some things you can't talk about,' said Waldo. 'They're not sacred, but they ought to be. Know what I mean?'

'No.'

'There she is now,' Waldo inclined his head towards the window, 'out there with someone and it doesn't matter who. That's how she is.'

'How is she?'

'She's tried it with you.'

'Tried what with me?'

'Haven't you twigged what she's after?'

'She isn't after me.'

Waldo pulled him round so that his back was towards the old woman who was now nodding and winking like clockwork. 'You're the one she wants. You know why.'

'Don't keep saying I know! I don't.'

'If she gets you she gets at me. That's what she really wants.'

'For God's sake!'

'You know why? She hates me.'

'You're crazy.'

'Wish I was. About that, anyway.'

[32]

Waldo's shoulders sagged. He looked, by luck and management, Jessel suspected, very tired.

Jessel said, 'You should have asked Plumley to come with you.'

Waldo's head jerked up. 'That's a foul thing to say. The foulest you could say.'

'According to *you*,' Jessel said, leaning on it, 'he's more her type than I am.'

'She's my *mother*!' Waldo, having also leaned, blinked furiously and dashed his hands over his eyes.

'I'm no use.' Jessel found it in him to add briskly, 'To either of you.'

'You promised to help.'

'I did not!'

'Trust you, you said.'

'I was fooling.'

'I'm not fooling.'

'What do you want me to do? Hold her while you stick a knife in?'

'Of course not. I'll see to that side of it.'

'How, for instance?'

'I'll make it look like an accident.'

'Naturally.'

'Dying's natural.'

'Murder isn't.'

'Yes it is, though. Animals do it all the time.'

'We're not animals.'

'It's not only here, you know. Everywhere we go, it's men, any man. Even that filthy old devil, Crau. You wouldn't credit that, would you?'

Crau was the husband of one of the witches, and the owner of the farm. An old man, but far from senile. It was not because of senility that he neither washed himself nor changed his clothes. He had the rank smell of a beast. Jessel who had seen him wolfing his food, lying dead drunk in the midden and thrashing children with a harness-strap, could believe that he also had the rank brutality.

'You know what she lets him do?'

'No!'

'You can guess, can't you?' Waldo frowned, then his brow lightened. 'I suppose you do know something?'

Jessel's knowledge on the general score was fairly exhaustive, though not empirical. He reckoned that Waldo would almost certainly have had practical experience.

'I know as much as you and a whole lot more. But I don't believe it about her.'

'Put yourself in my place. You can't ever say to yourself, now she's alone, she's quiet, now she's being my mother and nothing else. I've seen what she can get up to, and I tell you she can go pretty high.'

'Seen?'

'Yes. How would you like to watch your mother up to it?'

Jessel thought that it would be qualitatively more advanced than anything he had so far been obliged to witness his parents doing. 'I wouldn't talk about knocking her off if I did.'

'I just can't stand it any more.'

'Clear out, then.'

'And leave it going on? Don't you understand? I could never forget it. I've got to stop it!'

'O.K. Stop it.'

'I suppose your old man would hang me.' It took Jessel a moment to realise what he was talking about. 'Come to think of it, he couldn't. I'm a minor.'

Of course he would have it all worked out. He was working it out as he went along, he was getting it together. 'That's right. You're just a kid, and the kid thinks he can get away with murder.'

'Justifiable matricide. Your old dad would allow that.' Waldo was looking grave and balanced – as he had to be, seeing that he was on a knife-edge. 'I shan't try to get away. It will be up to someone to take up the burden of proof.'

Jessel began to realise that Waldo would appropriate any subject which he, Jessel, might want or purpose to make his own. Like the pretence that his father was a judge: Waldo was working it into the ground. Jessel yawned: yawning was easy, and honest. He yawned when he was hungry.

'Which is where you come in,' said Waldo. 'Look, don't worry, I'm not asking you to take part in the actual business. I'll handle that. What I want is an alibi. All you have to do is swear I was somewhere I wasn't at the material time. So that I couldn't have been where I was.'

'Where will that be?'

'Wherever they try to make out I was. We shan't know till it's done. You'll be an accessory after the fact.'

'Cut it out!'

'We're friends, aren't we?'

Jessel, who had wanted it said, turned and ran out of the house.

He walked to St Marcuse, five kilometres distant. The wind blew grit into his face. He was constantly fighting off thought of Mrs Klein. In the hour or so it took him to get to the village he had only about three non-consecutive minutes of not being fully and actually conscious of her. It made him wonder what he would do when he went back to school. Could he expect fifteen seconds' cognisance of algebra, physics or whatever, to every three hundred of Mrs Klein?

In St Marcuse he went to a café and ordered coffee and croissants. It should have been a nice experience sitting at a table on the pavement. The wind still blew, but in the shelter of the houses only enough to lift the grit into elegant spirals. People at the café sat drinking and talking and watching the spirals. People gestured and made spirals with their hands. He came out of his obsessive thoughts into the emancipated atmosphere like waking from a worrying dream. Then he spoilt it by wishing that Mrs Klein could see him sitting there.

As he walked back to La Bigorne he could taste salt in the air. He didn't need it to make him get the point. Tomorrow he would go home. There were three weeks of the holidays left and he would spend those as he always did, at Dollis Hill. He would prowl and cycle about. It would be perfectly in order, no one would question his right to be there, or mind if he was not. His bed and meals and laundry were arrangements to be kept in mind but not minded. He had money and his return ticket, he did not have to write that he was coming home and wait for a reply. There was bound to be someone in the house and it did not much matter who. At times like this, though this was the first time like this, he was glad of his independence, his scot-freeness.

I'll be going home tomorrow, he would say to Mrs Klein. He could sound casual but he had better be definite and he ought to sound sorry: I'm cut up about it and all that, but I'm afraid I have to go. If he told her while they were at supper he need not actually look at her, a glance in her general direction would be enough. It would indeed. She had a way of eclipsing. He had noticed that there was virtually nothing in her immediate vicinity unless she happened to be using or occupied with something, and then it existed merely to demonstrate how things could be done – cup lifted, spoon laid down, page turned, pebble dislodged – all with her purely personal touch. Actually, her direction was the reverse of general and he must try not to let his glance be held.

In the event, which came before supper time, his glance was held and fixed. There was a patch of ground between the farmyard and the house which had once been a garden. The goats ate everything that tried to grow, except for a massive shrub with oily leaves and a giant convulvulus with blue flowers the shape of gramophone horns. Jessel, on his way back from St Marcuse, looked over the wall. Mrs Klein was sitting in a carpet chair with a parasol over her shoulder. There was no sun, but the parasol was open, framing her face. Seeing that high, almost fraught pinkness superimposed on the grey silk of the parasol was disquieting. It disquieted Jessel: he felt his heart stop and re-start like a dud clock. He felt he had to concentrate to keep it ticking.

'James, come and talk to me.' She had asked right at the beginning did he like to be called James or Jimmy, she had said she wouldn't call him Jess, as Waldo did, she had said, 'It's not right for me,' and added seriously, 'I don't think Jimmy's right for you.' He had said he was called James at home, knowing even while he looked at her that he was seldom called anything there. Now she said, without irony, 'That is, if you have time to talk.' Her smile held no hint of rue. 'I know how little time there is to spare when one is young.'

He hoped she wouldn't take up the elderly theme again, he had made a fool of himself over that. He went unwillingly to stand beside her. She moved her feet which he now saw had been resting on a pumpkin. 'It was all I could find for a footstool. Now you can sit on it.'

'I'll stand.'

'Oh I can't keep looking up at you. Besides, it will bring you luck.'

'Luck?'

'It did for Cinderella.'

Gingerly, he lowered himself. The thing rolled under him, he squatted on it, knees apart, looking, as he was obliged to do, directly into her face.

Leaning down, she touched his cheek. He shivered. She was kind – and yes, she was tender. Didn't she know what she was doing? Didn't she know that even without the lifted finger she could make him make an unqualified idiot of himself?

'Don't you love it here? In the Midi? Even on a day like this – especially on a day like this! All those hot blue days we remember as one hot blue day without end. But this is something else. I shall remember every moment of today.' So would he, starting with the moment when he had sat and puked in the boat. 'The first thing I heard when I woke this morning was that marvellous sound – Listen!' She held out her hand, cupped, as if to catch and hold something. 'What does it remind you of?' He couldn't hear anything, and said so. 'Really no? Of course some people can't, or won't. Waldo, for instance. But you, I would have thought you would. Oh do try, just listen.' She put her head on one side, inclining it towards

[37]

the ground. He supposed the wind was scraping about among the dry grasses but he was too mightily aware of the figure he was cutting to try to listen. 'It's like someone coming,' she said, 'the moment before you turn and see who it is.' He kept still, not even nodding. 'It's the sound of someone's skin when they're very close. You know? You must have waited for someone, you must have heard it.' He sat on the damned pumpkin and gaped. His mouth went dry with gaping. She sighed, and now there was more than a hint of rue in her smile. 'Tell me what you've been doing.'

'We went fishing. Waldo did. He caught a tiger-shark. Or so he said. That's what he said it was. Of course I didn't believe him.' Perhaps he shouldn't have said 'of course', he was forgetting that Waldo was her son. 'I think, actually, it's pretty unlikely.' Seeing a slight lift of her brows he said firmly, 'In fact it's tommyrot.'

'And you? What did you do?'

'I didn't fish. I don't like messing about.'

'Nor I.'

'He brought the fish back for supper. It's black, with teeth. It could be poisonous.'

'I shouldn't dream of eating it.'

He blushed. It was as if he and not Waldo had proposed to kill her. In jest or earnest it had been proposed and he was remembering it at this moment. Looking at her, and remembering, he went hot with shame and horror and a fearful unresolved longing.

She said languidly, 'Tell me what you do.'

'Do?'

'All day. It's obvious what I do.' She twirled the parasol on her shoulder. It went round and round behind her head, faster and faster. 'I sit and read or doze, or wander along the road. Or I talk to Waldo. If it couldn't be seen what I do, it could be surmised. But you're such a private person. I can't surmise what you do.'

He said stiffly, 'Cycle or walk to the village or to the sea and take a boat out. We went to the Cascadière caves yesterday.'

'What do you do when you're by yourself?'

He was bemused by the spinning of the parasol. The immediate world as he understood it, or rather, failed to understand it, went round and round. Mrs Klein, Waldo, La Bigorne and the morning's scummy sea and sky were mixing and creaming and blending. He knew that he would not now be able to isolate them and sort out what had happened, was still happening. And those were the days when he was young and green enough to suppose that people and things could be totally independent of each other.

'I have to go home tomorrow.'

'Tomorrow? It's rather sudden, isn't it?' She sounded surprised. No more than that. If he had hoped for more he was put in his place. To show that he knew it, he said, 'I hope it won't be inconvenient, I don't expect it will matter really.'

'Is anything wrong? Is it your parents?'

'No.'

'Of course they must want to see something of you before the end of the holidays.' He nodded and she said, 'We shall miss you.' A collective 'we': as well as herself and Waldo it included the Craus, the tiny – totally negligible – deprivations his absence would mean.

A girl employed to look after him when he was very young had said, as she was leaving, 'I shall miss you.' She spoke forcefully, she was a forceful girl, with a habit of knuckling the back of his head. He readily understood, at five years of age, that it was the back of his head she would miss.

'I know I shall,' said Mrs Klein. She stopped spinning her parasol, took it off her shoulder and furled it with one beautiful turn of her wrist. 'Waldo's friends are usually grubby little boys.'

Nothing more was said between them. At that juncture nothing more was possible. She gave him to reflect on what he might have missed. He fled, muttering something about having to pack. He heard Waldo's voice as he ran, and slipped into the barn to avoid him.

Remembering Mrs Klein was going to be a full-time occupation.

At sixteen he had not had much experience of memory. He supposed it to be infallible, he knew it was implacable, an endless replay,
plus unconcluded and inconclusive analyses and crazy speculations.
He saw no prospect of forgetting, even for one hundred and eighty
seconds out of every hour.

And yet, what had she actually done that was so memorable? She
had looked and smiled and sat at table and walked on the grass and
inquired was he enjoying himself and touched his hand. Things that
everybody did, except touching him, all the time. Of course it wasn't
what she did, but the way she did it, the way she did everything.
Which to her meant what it had to mean at the time, and no more.
Like picking up a cup to drink and spreading her toes. And
tenderness was as much a part of her as her pinkness, probably her
pinkness was evidence of her tenderness. She was a tender person.
She was a lover of the world and he, in common with every other
creature which was not openly and obviously disgusting, had had a
share of it.

Already he was analysing and concluding. He thought furiously,
you total idiot! And looked to where the cobwebs hung in ropes in
the darkest corner of the barn. How many years had it taken for those
webs to form? How many spiders had spun them? How many flies
been caught? Had she ever looked on these dirty things? No, she
wouldn't come here, she would have no cause to, not even out of
curiosity. She asked questions not from curiosity but out of her love
of the world.

The barn was a squalid place. He began to walk around it, picking
his way over piles of rusted chains, blades, cogs, broken unidenti-
fiable things, tubs dyed purple with grape juice and smelling of fust,
rubble of smashed roof tiles. It was a hapless, hopeless place. But as
soon as he thought that, he asked was he thinking so because she
hadn't been there? Waldo had told him that it was used for family
gatherings, weddings and funeral parties. 'I saw a kneesup in there
once when old Crau's wife died.' 'A what?' 'Well,' said Waldo,
grinning, 'they don't much marry but they sometimes snuff it.' So

the barn was not entirely abandoned by people, and anyway the animals, the goats and hens and mules, used it all the time. And the dogs. He could hear the jaws of one of them snapping at flies.

The farm dogs were skinny, hysterical brutes and he braced himself for the inevitable outburst of barking and snarling when his presence was sensed. Then he realised that there was another dimension to the snapping sound. Several other dimensions. It took him no time at all to recall what they were. In the semi-dark he almost kicked over Waldo's bait-bucket. The fish, the ugly black thing, was still jumping in it. The sound was the sound he had heard in the dimensions of the boat and the sea and Waldo. And Mrs Klein. The fish was part, the farcical part, of the same arraignment.

It wasn't jumping with the persistence it had shown at first. It was just rearing up and falling back with a noise like a fish falling into a bucket. It was a fact that a thing sounded like itself, and only like itself. The notion of there being dimensions was rot, and although his stomach turned and his heart with it, he forced himself to look. He said, it's a fish, half dead, in a bucket of water, nothing else. She is not remotely connected with it and as of this moment I am not remotely connected with her.

If it hadn't been so far he would have taken it back to the beach and thrown it into the sea. He wasn't sentimental about animals, they had a place in the scheme of things but he wouldn't have cared if they lost it. He simply didn't like waste. The fish wasn't going to be eaten and if it had another function it might as well be serving that function. However, it was too far to the beach. He found a piece of sacking and dropped it over the bucket.

The Kleins had their supper at the same time as the family. There was no pretence of La Bigorne being a guest-house. It was a farm and whether the Craus worked it or not they lived to farm workers' routine. The evening meal was at six and anyone who did not eat then went without. Mrs Klein had once told Jessel that the original arrangement was for the Kleins to take their meals with the Craus, in the farmhouse kitchen. She had said, smiling, 'I was obliged to discourage it. The company I keep at meals is as important to me as the meal itself.'

On that last evening he would have said that the company was more important. She didn't look as if she could, or ever would need to put food into her mouth, chew and salivate and swallow. There was absolutely no indication that she had digestive processes. She wore black, a devastating change from her usual pastel colours. Jessel dared not look openly or long, he had to keep pulling his eyes away from the place where her throat went into a kind of lattice and the flesh re-emerged beneath, scrupulously brimming out of little lozenges of black silk. It was something he might have expected had he thought about it. But had he thought, he could not in a million years have expected it. It was definitely beautiful and potentially ugly: it could be a fluke but he knew it wasn't. It was enormously significant. It was a kind of code.

'Where have you been?' said Waldo. 'I looked for you under every stone.'

'I went for a walk.'

'Where to?'

'St Marcuse.'

'You're not here to go mooning about on your own, you're here to keep me company.' Jessel was not lost for a retort but he could not make it because of her. 'That's one purpose of the exercise. The other you know.'

'Don't tease,' said Mrs Klein.

'Going off like that was an unfriendly act.'

Waldo looked hurt. It was patently a contrivance and much overdone. Jessel, who would have punched him had they been alone, filled his mouth with bread.

'Loneliness is a disease,' said Mrs Klein. 'I've always been afraid of catching it.' Jessel looked steadfastly into his plate. 'But it isn't contagious, is it?' She spoke to him as if they two were alone and having a private conversation. 'It's not a disease we pick up, we're born with the germ inside us and it starts to be active the minute we're born. It's in the flesh.' He looked up. 'I have never believed in the marriage of true minds.' Her smile was essentially for him. He was, as usual, mystified. At the same time he thought he detected privilege. She intended him to understand and whatever was missing it was up to him to supply.

'Tomorrow we'll go to the hellhole at Emonde,' said Waldo. 'Le Trou de L'Enfer. It's an underground grotto with a lake and stalactites and mummies left over from the stone age.'

'James is going home tomorrow.'

'What?' Waldo's head came up as if he had been hit under the chin.

'His parents have sent for him.'

'Rot. He hasn't had a letter since he came here.'

'James?' It was a gentle reminder that it was his turn to say something.

'He's a rotten liar.'

'Why should he lie?'

'Why do you want to go?' Waldo asked him.

'Perhaps he's not happy.' She maintained the privacy of their conversation, talked directly to him over Waldo's head, out of Waldo's reach.

'I don't want to go, I have to.' That was true in essence and the essence was all that was needful. The rest, the real reason, it was his duty to conceal. Out of respect for her, and out of pity. Yes, he thought, he had cause to be sorry for her. 'It's been very nice here.'

'You're not going,' said Waldo.

'Who's to stop me?'

'I will. What the hell do you think I'll do here on my own?'

'Fool around, like you always do.'

Waldo leaned over, tapped on the table. 'I haven't finished with you yet.'

'He has finished with you,' Mrs Klein said to him.

'Tell us why you want to go.'

'That's my business.'

'But you see,' said Waldo, enormously reasonable, 'it's not. In your case it's common politeness to tell us. You're our guest and you owe us an explanation.'

At that moment one of the younger Crau men came and stood in the doorway. He was short and stocky, with black curling hair and a beard which grew in ringlets along his jaw. The hair on his chest curled out of the neck of his dirty singlet. His trousers were stained poignant blue. So far as Jessel could see he had no reason to be there, except to stare at Mrs Klein, which he did, leaning against the door and combing his beard with his fingers. She gazed back at him. Once she shut her eyes and slowly opened them as if taking in and digesting the sight.

Then the man – Louis, Babert, Gilles, whatever he was called – turned and went. Mrs Klein drank some wine.

'I'll tell you why he's going.' Waldo had reddened, the colour was fiercest in his ears, he was staring across the table to the door where Louis or Babert or Gilles had been. 'It's nothing to do with his parents, I don't believe he's got any. He was put together from a blueprint.'

'At least I'm organised.'

'He hasn't had a letter.'

'There are other ways of communicating,' said Jessel.

'Like thought transference?'

'If people are close enough,' said Mrs Klein.

But it was no longer a private conversation. She was giving what there was of it a minimum of her attention, about the same degree and kind as she would allow a small animal that was getting under her feet.

'I got a telegram,' said Jessel.

'Show us.'

'I threw it away.'

'For your information, they haven't invented telegrams here yet. They signal with drums.'

Waldo was now watching his mother and it occurred to Jessel that

[44]

he was trying to say something private to her. It was doubtful if she was listening. She had stretched out one arm on the table and was scrutinising the inside of her elbow.

Whereas Jessel was used to being floored – for him it was the reverse of the coin, any coin – Waldo was quite unprepared. He looked almost comic in his dismay. He snatched up a spoon and Jessel thought he was about to hit his mother. 'You're the reason he's going!'

Brandishing the spoon, he looked wholly comic but Jessel did not laugh.

Mrs Klein glanced up from her elbow. 'I am?'

'He's scared stiff I'm going to kill you. And that I'll make him help me.'

'Shut up!' Jessel, launching himself across the table to reach Waldo, knocked over her glass of wine. The stain sank into the softish scrubbed wood.

She took up the salt-cellar and sprinkled salt. 'It's what one does for linen.'

Jessel found the remark obscure, but so was everything. It was the most obscure moment of his life.

She said, 'Why should he think that?'

He couldn't get up and walk out because of the way she was looking at him, holding him in obscurity. Not one feature of her face had a clear meaning. He could only stare with increasing foolishness, feeling it increase until his every act, future and past, was open to question. And the question was the one she was asking now.

Waldo leaned over and stroked her nose with his thumb. It was ungentle but she submitted, smiling. To Jessel it signified ownership, and familiarity. He was deeply shocked by the familiarity, which was of a kind he did not yet know how to dream of.

'Because, darling Skeeter, he thinks you're lovers with Babert and Gilles and Rizzo and Louis and the old man. With all the Craumagnons, in fact.'

'Oh my dear.' She turned to Jessel and in her face was a pure enjoyment. He could see no sign of impurity, and that was the greatest ambiguity. It was quite beyond his comprehension. The enjoyment was being shared with Waldo, but not like a cake or a joke, it was more like flesh sharing blood.

III

Mrs Poole was finding her feet. She had visited other offices in the Corporation and brought back executive images which she transferred to Jessel. He found absurd and humiliating the import she attached to his every move. She adopted a kind of hushed vigilance, poised not so much to obey his wishes as to forestall them. Her strenuous efforts to read his mind threatened to interfere with the working of it.

When he rang through to the outer office he was aware that it was not a time to be leaving his desk, too late for lunch, too early for tea, but it was not a time he would wait beyond. It was positively the last moment. His hand went to the intercom at exactly a quarter past three and his voice said, 'I am going out.'

'You've got the Finance Committee at five.'

'I shall be back by then.'

'You want to read the minutes?'

'Thank you, no. But it was a provident thought.' Providently, too, in view of his imminent retirement, he was endeavouring to wind down. What point was there in clinging on to threads when he soon must drop the whole tapestry?

'I thought you'd want to be oh fate. Up to the minute, like.' She was probably expecting him to join her in her smile.

He said, 'Fay.'

'Excuse me?'

'The "t" is not sounded in the French.' He saw as plainly as if she was before him the colour rush up her neck as if a switch had been thrown. Or knocked on.

He hurried out with the idea of seeing the last of her blushes. If only he could be sure it was the last, or that she would learn to discriminate between what was mortifying and what was not. He might delicately have to intimate, for it was more important for her to know that order of priority than any other. His colleagues had noticed her propensity and were calling her 'Poppy Poole' and she, poor child, thought it was evidence of how well she was fitting in and blushed with pleasure.

He hailed a taxi. 'The Nekrassic Box Company.'

'Eh?' said the man.

The name of Waldo's firm had been on the tip of his tongue, but not the address. He had been obliged to look for that in the telephone directory. 'Lillybrae Street, Walworth.'

'Where?'

'Walworth's the other side of the river –'

'Look,' said the man, without patience, 'this Nebraski Box –'

'Nekrassic.'

'– is it the Elephant end or the Surrey Canal end?'

'I'm sorry, I don't know.'

The man sighed and pulled away from the kerb. Jessel thought it worth noting, in some respect or other, that he would only have had to name the corporation he worked for, or give its initials, for the driver to know where its headquarters were. In fact, the building that housed it was the orientation point for that area of London.

In Lillybrae Street, which had never seen a lily or a brae, there was an open conduit in the middle of the road. It looked insanitary. The buildings were windowless, with well-kicked doors. The taxi-driver went the short length of the street but they saw no names or numbers, only some hackneyed graffiti.

'You sure it's Nebraski?'

'Leave me here,' said Jessel. 'I'll find it.'

He did eventually locate a board high on a wall. 'Angel Nekrassor', it claimed, 'box-maker to the world.' An arrow pointed along a passage. He thought, there's no access, how can they load? The answer was almost certainly to be seen in the walls of the passage-way which were deeply scored, in places the bricks were cut to their yellow cores. Everything had to be manhandled to the road. At the end of the passage was an open door. A panel bore the words 'Nekrassic Elegante' and the outlines of a box tied with a bow.

Jessel was shocked. He had always supposed that Waldo worked at a good address, for a good sound company with a standing which, though not universal like his own, was at least as morally acceptable. He had even felt that being so much smaller and its motivation so much simpler – simply to make and market boxes – there was less danger of its reputation being tarnished. There was, he had believed, integrity and dignity in small firms which were in danger of being lost in the multinationals.

Beyond the open door was a flight of stairs. No commissionaire, no hall-porter, not even a hall. The stairs, uncarpeted, went directly up to a landing with doors opening off. On one, words had been hand-lettered, three letters to a panel, and Jessel puzzled for a full minute by what process of manufacture boxes had to be unfrozen before he realised that the words were not two but one: 'Office'. On another door the word 'Private' had been split less equally, but it was from a third, unidentified door that a girl emerged to the brisk convulsion and roar of descending water, a scant gallon which ceased to descend even as she adjusted her dress. Without compunction she zipped up her skirt and promptly unzipped it again.

'Yes?' she said, examining the fastener.

'I'm looking for Mr Waldo Klein.'

'He's not here.'

Jessel, who had had the situation in view before he came, asked to speak to whoever was handling Waldo's work.

'I am.'

'You?'

'What there is.'

She was still bent over, fiddling with her zip, and Jessel asked himself who had given him his ideas about Waldo's job. Definitely not Waldo. Without actually being a scoundrel, or technically outside the law, Waldo had little use for probity, public or private,

[49]

except to take what advantage of it he could. And having himself no need of dignity he was unconscious of it as a requisite in anyone or anything else. He seldom talked about his work or the people he worked with. He seldom talked about himself and his affairs, having mastered the art of seeming to exist in a vacuum, outside all but the basic considerations of needing to eat and sleep and make a living. He referred to Nekrassor as 'the little Greek' and Jessel pictured the man as childlike and wholly dependent on Waldo's business sense.

'Do you know where he is?'

'No,' she said, straightening and looking at him at last. 'And I'm cheesed off being asked.'

'I'm sorry –'

'How should I know? But everyone thinks I should.'

'I beg your pardon. I just hoped you might – that he might –'

'I wasn't in his pocket.'

Jessel decided that it was the fact she resented rather than the idea. 'Nor I,' he said, 'though I'm a very old friend of his. Perhaps no one was, in that way.'

'What way?'

'I meant in that sense.'

'I'm asking, what sense?'

He felt like a poor swimmer in a heavy sea. 'He didn't – doesn't – give confidences. He takes them. Even so, there must be someone who has some idea where he is.'

'Why must there be?'

'He couldn't just vanish.'

'He did. He went to lunch and never came back. That was weeks ago.' Jessel looked at the door marked 'Private'. 'I'd like to see Mr Nekrassor.'

'We phoned the police and the hospitals and Mrs Klein. In case he'd been run over or mugged or gone off with another woman. No one knew anything.'

'Perhaps Mr Nekrassor –'

'He's not here.'

'Who is here?' said Jessel, without sarcasm. He was thinking there must be a next in the chain of management, next to Waldo, now next to Nekrassor. 'I mean, is there someone I could talk to about Mr Klein?'

'You're doing as well as can be expected with me.' She threw open the door marked 'Office' and called within, 'Here's a very old friend of Waldo's who thinks we ought to know where he is.'

'Oh no, I don't think that –'

'Come in, very old friend,' said the girl. 'Talk to anyone you like.'

There were two people in the room, a man and a boy. The man was youngish and fat, the boy was a skinhead and had the biggest teeth Jessel had ever seen. They protruded from his jaw like a cowcatcher on a train.

The girl sat down at a desk and started pounding away at a typewriter. The fat man looked thoughtfully at Jessel and Jessel, averting his eyes from the wretched boy's teeth, looked round the room.

There was just space for people to move between the desks and cabinets and the stacks of cardboard and a table spread with cups and a jar of instant coffee and an electric kettle. There were two windows looking on to smoked bricks which time and weather had peeled to show their sulphurous core. The shelves that went up to the ceiling were crammed with box-files and parcels of papers with elaborately curled edges ranging in colour from pale biscuit to ironmould. There was a potent atmosphere, a mix of the material and immaterial factors obtaining in that room to which everyone and everything must have contributed. Yes, must, thought Jessel, for it was irreducibly complex and domestic. He had, thank heavens, never encountered anything like it before. How curious, then, that it was immediately recognisable, almost remembered. He would like to have sunk through the floor into the passage below, and to walk out without the necessity of saying a further word.

The girl stopped typing to dig her thumb in the air. 'That's his desk.'

[51]

It was in a corner, back to the window, facing the door, probably the best position in the room. A heavy old anglepoise lamp leaned over it. Two wire baskets were full of paper and a White Horse Whisky ashtray brimmed with stubs. A piece of igneous rock, just like any other piece of igneous rock, lay to one side of the blotter.

'You're welcome to look for clues.'

The fat man said, 'My name's Inchcape. Did he mention me?'

The boy opened his jaws. They made an explosive sound and the prominent thyroid cartilage in his throat moved up and down.

Jessel shuddered. 'He doesn't discuss his business affiliations.'

The boy took the teeth out of his mouth and dropped them on his desk. He grinned at Jessel. 'Joke chompers. When I get them properly plugged in I can bite with them.'

Jessel felt the warmth come back quickly, too quickly, to his face. 'My name's Jessel, James Jessel. I've known Mr Klein from boyhood.'

'He never mentioned you,' said the fat man.

Waldo's desk had not been dusted, and there was a far from fine film over the papers and greasy finger-marks – Waldo's? – on the wood. The papers were bills of lading, old invoices, not current memorabilia.

'What about his diary?'

'What about it?'

'Didn't keep one,' said the boy.

'He didn't keep anything,' said the girl.

'May I?' They watched Jessel go to the desk and move the papers aside. Instinctively he rubbed the tips of his fingers together. He was looking for some sign, something to enlighten him. He badly needed enlightenment. Detectives found words, numbers, significant doodles on blotting-pads. Waldo's pad had no blotting-paper in it.

'He sponged,' said the girl, typing again.

'Sponged?'

'By the end of the month he was a sweet honey of a sponge.'

'He even sponged on Chris.'

The boy nodded. 'Still owes me.'

'If there's anything outstanding of course I will –' Jessel's hand moved to his breast-pocket.

'Fifty pee.' The boy giggled.

'Until he can settle matters himself I shall be glad to reimburse you.' They looked at him unfriendlily. There was no reason why they should feel friendliness. 'I hope you will allow me, on his behalf –' Jessel reached into his pocket but could not, while they were all staring, bring out his wallet. It was too cold-blooded. He remained with his hand on his breast.

The girl stopped typing. 'You think he'll come back then?'

'Of course.'

'Jeeze yes,' said the boy.

The fat man sighed. The girl said, 'Why did he go?'

Jessel looked again at Waldo's desk. He could not think of anywhere else to look. If there was a reason, anything he could accept as a reason, it should surely have left its mark on that desk. He had only to recognise it.

'What's his wife like?'

Jessel said sharply, 'That is not the reason, I assure you. Absolutely not.' But it could be that he himself had, for being sure, quite another reason from the one he was giving, or intimating, to them.

'I seen her,' said the boy. 'She came here after Waldo went. Nekrassor took her out to lunch. She asked me if I worked with Waldo and I said I worked right next to him.' He picked up the joke teeth and fitted them into his mouth.

Jessel took a fifty-pence piece out of his purse. 'Are you sure this is all he owes you?'

The boy grinned painfully and salivated round the teeth. 'He left me this on account.' He held up a French franc.

He went back to his office and rang Connie. 'I think I should go and see Daisy Klein this evening.'

'And Waldo.'

'Waldo has gone away. If you remember.'

'I remember, but I daresay he's back home by now.' She dared say, she was unconcerned, blithe, and there was no reason – apart from his own concern – for her to be otherwise. 'It's the sort of thing he'd do, go off without a word and come back when it suits him and not give a damn about anyone.'

He was aware of his lips tightening in something as ungenuine but a little stronger than the ghost of a smile. 'On Daisy's behalf he would expend all the damnation he was capable of.'

'What?'

'I was continuing in your idiom.'

'Why don't you ring up and ask if he's back?'

'And if he's not?'

'You don't have to go. Unless you want to see her.'

'I daresay I shall find it rather distressing. But to ask over the telephone seems too casual and impersonal. I think I should go.'

'It's not as if you can *do* anything.'

'I shall be about an hour.' He hung up with the feeling of one whose concerns are not recognised.

It occurred to him, at the moment he looked through the glass of the door in Bismarck Road, and before any hand had appeared to open it, that Daisy knew where her husband was. Of course, she had known all along. He looked through the amber and wine-coloured glass and his spirit warmed, expanded. In due time all would be explained.

She must either think him a credulous fool or over-discreet. She wasn't likely to give him the benefit of the doubt. She would derive amusement from his dismay. His going to Waldo's office asking questions would entertain anyone who happened to be in the know; he was probably the only one who was not.

He rang the bell. The coloured glass had become deceptive and irresponsible, appropriate to the circumstances. Exactly what those were, he might surmise. All might be explained, but by no means all would be acceptable. There were more than one set of inferences to be drawn from his visit to Waldo's box company. Leaving aside those which other people might draw about himself, there were some indisputable ones he could draw about the condition of the business.

Daisy opened the door. She held up her cheek for his salutation but turned away before he could give it. The top of her head buffeted his nose and caused his eyes to water.

She moved in a kind of scramble, shoulders, elbows and her inconsiderable thighs brushing against the furniture. There was a sense of uncontainment and he was as suddenly sure that Waldo was not here as he had been that he was.

'Is there no news?' he called, quite sharply, to her back. She stopped, holding aside the bead curtain for him. It was an unwonted act of courtesy: in all the time he had been coming here he had not seen anyone, except Connie, regard the beads as an obstacle. One simply passed through them. He took the beads from her, let them drop. He heard their usual finalising click.

The sitting-room looked ransacked. Chairs and tables which to his certain knowledge had stayed in the same places for years were now moved, not to new ones, but randomly skewed and pushed aside. One chair was turned to face the wall. The doors of the sideboard were ajar, a drawer was pulled out, books dropped open on their spines. The hearthrug was rucked, dangerously he thought, and stooped to straighten it.

'Don't.'

She had not answered his question. She was in no condition to. He feared he had provoked her, she might have been more restrained if he had not asked. Should he have asked anything? Should he have avoided the subject of Waldo, gleaned what he could, gone away advanced only by the demolishing of his second thoughts and with no new ones to replace them?

Daisy dropped into a chair and sat sideways with her legs over the arm. It was a lax, unco-ordinated attitude. There had been a change in her appearance since the last time he saw her. She was now rather dark whereas he thought of her as being fair. Her hair, skin and lips were varying degrees of the same brown. Her clothes had never been good, but the way she had worn them they had seemed a functional extension of herself. Now they were coverings put on out of habit. He suspected that she did not take them off at night.

'Have you come to supper?' He shook his head. 'Good. There's nothing to eat.'

'I hope you have proper meals.'

'I eat like a horse. Why do we say that? The only horse I ever knew was a dainty eater. It liked soft-boiled eggs and French peaches.'

She had not asked him to sit down. He was not accustomed to wait for an invitation but she was occupying his usual chair.

'Have you heard anything?' Connie would say she had let herself go. But go where? 'I wondered if – I thought he might have come back.'

'He?'

It was too much. He said sharply, 'I am inclined to wonder if he ever went away.'

'Inclined to wonder?' Her eyes filled with tears. To his relief they did not fall, she kept them between her eyelids.

'I'm sorry. One tends to think of all the possibilities on these occasions.' He thought, vexed, that it was scarcely an occasion, it was neither a wedding nor a funeral, it was nothing definite. 'I had to find out if there was any – development. We're going away on Saturday.'

'You and Connie?' She did not wait for him to answer. 'Lucky old Connie.' She might be mocking him. On the other hand she had reason to be envious. 'I don't believe in luck. I believe you pay for what you get. After you get it or before, you pay.'

He allowed her bitterness and found himself saying, out of some reservation of his own, 'Connie takes things to heart.'

'Help yourself to a drink.'

'Perhaps a small sherry. Will you join me?'

She shook her head. He had noticed, and framed his preference accordingly, that there was only a bottle of sweet sherry in evidence. No spirits.

[56]

While he was pouring it she said, 'I've been to look at some bodies.'

'What?'

'They have a general description and they asked me to look at some possibles.'

'They?'

'The police.'

He said, appalled, 'They might have spared you that.'

'They couldn't. Who else knows his body?'

He put the bottle down. Sherry seemed wrong at this juncture. And he no longer wanted it. 'Did you –'

'Oh I knew.' He hadn't been going to ask that, he was trying to think of some way of letting her see that he shared her distress and had his own. 'I knew that none of them was him. They had come from the river – the Pool of London.' She folded up, neatly as a penknife and sat on her feet with her hands tucked into her armpits. He felt that now she did it for warmth and whatever comfort she could get. 'Water – and the police said rats – do alter people.'

'Why should they think that Waldo –' he essayed, mistakenly, and too late to stop it, a grimace – 'has gone into the Pool of London?'

She made the same sort of face, but on her it was a grin of pain. 'Of course it's not the last thing he'd do. But they don't know him and they don't go much on character. The odd thing was, on one of the bodies was something I recognised.'

'What was it?'

'Shirts aren't so special nowadays, they can come from department stores, anywhere. But this one had my sewing on it. My sewing isn't special either, except specially bad. I could swear it was one of my cobble-ups. I didn't swear it to the police. They're so awfully keen to close the case.'

Now it was Jessel who felt cold, bleak to the bone at the thought of false concepts cheerfully entertained, even favoured. Death by drowning would be such a quick, simple dispensation. 'But the man wasn't Waldo?'

[57]

'Not the one I saw, the one they said was wearing the shirt with my sewing on when they fished him out of the water.'

'If it wasn't Waldo but it was Waldo's shirt –'

'It was Waldo's shirt.'

'Then how –'

'If he bought new clothes and threw away his own, a vagrant – any vagrant – could find the shirt and put it on.'

'Why should he throw away his clothes?'

'So as not to be traced.'

'Traced?'

'Have you seen Nekrassor?'

'No, but I've been to his office, his and Waldo's.'

'Nekrassor paid his salary.'

'I thought – I understood Waldo had a half share in the business.'

'You've seen the business, what use would a half share be in that, even if he had it?'

'I thought it was a flourishing concern.' He had thought that it was brilliantly, sometimes comically mismanaged, but always with Continental flair: with some clever, not to say sharp, dealing, and well diversified, not to say devious, interests. 'I understood, I was given to understand, that they controlled the market in boxes.'

'The market in boxes! Nekrassor is bankrupt and Waldo has disappeared and there's something between them which the police would like to bury or burn or drown or otherwise see the back of.'

'I don't understand you.'

'They showed me a black man for my husband.'

'That must have been a mistake –'

'Someone opened the wrong drawer. Oh yes.' She unlocked her arms, put up her fists before her face as if she were about to swear an oath. 'I tell you they're not interested. They have better things to do.'

'Your precious Waldo', Connie had said once, and Jessel had felt obliged, because her resentment might be justified, to examine the value he put on him. He had got as far as classifying theirs as an association rather than a friendship, the associating being all on his side. What guarantee, what intimation did he have that Waldo associated him with anyone or anything? Except, possibly, a fish. Thinking of Jessel did he think, and smile, of a black reptilian creature jumping in a bucket? 'Did you bring in the police or did Nekrassor?'

'Are you mad? The best thing that can happen is that they don't find him.'

'Will Nekrassor bring charges?'

'There'll be no one to charge if Waldo keeps away.'

'Is there nothing I can do to help?'

'You can't help him because you don't know where he is and the only way you can help me is to bring him back and that wouldn't be helping him.'

He said, appealing to the gods or fate, some recognisable authority, on both their behalves, 'Shall we ever know what happened?'

She levered herself out of the chair. Sitting in it had become intolerable. Stillness, she made it plain, was torture. 'He threw away his clothes and the tramp who found his shirt and put it on got drunk or doped and fell in the river and drowned.'

'It's feasible.'

'It's what I'm settling for.'

He said, with the idea of consoling her, 'And for what he gave you.'

'He gave me hell. What did he give you?'

'I think – a sense of place.'

If she saw the irony she did not acknowledge it. She seized the chair, in which he had been wont to sit, and pulled it towards her and immediately thrust it away again. 'It's not what you get or what you hoped to get, it's not what you settle for that matters. It's settling – for anything or for nothing – that's what's important.' She went on pulling and pushing, again and again, working at it – or rather, he thought, as if she was bad-naturedly playing with the chair.

[59]

IV

'I used to think that. I used to think that if I hadn't said yes when I was asked, if I'd said let me think it over, try again tomorrow, I'd have had a different life. I didn't care, I was too scared no one would ask me twice.'

'Oh heavens.' Connie laughed.

'Now I've stopped wishing for other lives. I just want the old one back.' There was a pregnant pause. Connie straightened her face and waited for the birth. 'I hope you'll never know what it is to be alone.'

Connie had heard someone speak that line on television the previous evening. She remembered the play as being mostly devoted to shots of naked couples reeling and writhing in bed, with an enhancement of distorting mirrors. Connie had been bothered not by the passion, which would have had her sympathy had it been real, but by the knowledge that the actors were having to act it. She kept wondering how often they had had to rehearse and if they ever got carried away and to hell with the cameras.

'Do you ever think about it?' said Edith.

Once, when Jim was taking out insurance and someone said, 'In the event of your pre-deceasing your husband', Connie had realised that dying was something she was going to have to do by herself. 'I try not to. There's no point.'

'You don't think about anything!'

'Why are we having this conversation?'

'You don't appreciate what you've got. Here you are, still one of a pair when most of us are widowed or divorced or just ditched, with a kind, marriage-abiding husband who's willing and able to take you to the south of France and all you do is gripe.'

'I said I'd like to be *asked*. That's all.'

'Is there some other place you'd like to go?'

'I don't care where we go. It's the principle, being taken for granted.'

'I'd even jump at the chance of being taken for a ride.'

Edith was exaggerating, as she always did. She was a swiper where a flick would do. She had hosts of friends, male as well as female, and was escorted all over the place. If Connie were to point that out she would say it wasn't the same. The same as what! In a small spirit of exasperation Connie declared, 'We don't like to do the same things, Jim and I. He likes walking in the country; if we go into the town he falls asleep on his feet. I said what on earth will he do in Antibes and he said he'd take the car and drive into the hills. "You'll be happy with the beach and the shops," he said.'

'Well, you will.'

'It's not exactly a shared experience.'

'Who gets that, at our age?'

'If I'd married someone else I'd have turned out differently.' She was as certain of that as of the fact that she lived and breathed. But now that she had, so to speak, turned out, there was no chance of her changing.

'You'd never have liked walking.' Edith, losing interest, got up and battered about in search of cigarettes.

Connie, who had given it thought, persisted. 'The thing is, I've had to be unlike Jim – even more than I really am – I've had to be as unlike as I could. I'd have been no one otherwise. When we were first married I tried to go along with everything he said and did, think the same thoughts, look at things the same way. I wanted never to give him a moment's cause for alarm. But I couldn't keep it up, I couldn't pretend. Not for so long, not for nearly long enough. It had to be all night as well as all day.'

Edith, in the act of putting her thumb through the cellophane of a new pack of cigarettes, looked up sharply. 'What?'

'It came down to that. It would, wouldn't it? He's so consistent.'

'You mean you had to pretend sex when you didn't want it?'

'No.' Connie was amused at her own candour. She did not wish Jim to be misunderstood but she no longer minded herself being understood. It was one of the rare advantages of getting old. 'It was the other way round. I had to pretend I didn't want it.'

Edith hooted. 'I've said it before and I say it again, you don't know how lucky you are. Jim's the salt of the earth. Take a pinch whenever you can.'

For one thing, she didn't like flying. It might have occurred to him when he was making his arrangements, all of them without reference to her – the place, the time, the hotel, the very idea of a holiday which he had picked up where they had left it earlier in the year. He hadn't asked would she rather go by train and sea. Not that they flew all that often. But as she said, each time the subject came up, it didn't seem natural.

Walking beside him into Heathrow as he manoeuvred their luggage trolley which had googly wheels, she said, 'I thought we were going by car.'

'There's been a change of plan. You're rather late noticing.'

'You're rather late telling me!'

'We agreed it was more economical to hire a car at the other end. And less fraught.'

'Not for me. For me it's one big fraught.' An enormously fat woman passed them tugging a mountain of pigskin suitcases. 'Oh heavens, *she's* not going up, is she?'

'We'll only be an hour and a half in the air.'

'If we ever get in the air! Isn't there a weight check?'

'They weigh the baggage.'

'What about the passengers? Even a feather falls to the ground. When you think about it –' she was thinking, appalled – 'there's no way we can stay up.'

'There is. Aerodynamics.'

'Why couldn't we go by sea?'

'It takes too long.'

'Too long for what?'

'We have ten days' holiday and I don't intend to spend four of them travelling.' The trolley, despite his efforts, was bearing away diagonally. 'We seem to have chosen a more than usually recalcitrant machine.' Connie watched him crouch down to fiddle with the wheels. She noted, not for the first time, the polish – it was a glitter – of skull under his thinning hair. 'Don't they ever service these things?' He looked up, smiling. 'My dear, you need not worry – they definitely do service the planes.'

Connie walked on, caught up and passed the fat woman. She had only been peeved before, but now she didn't see, she honestly didn't, why she should be obliged to do this ridiculous thing. It was not what the birds did, not that marvellous speciality, it was a violation of the law of gravity, achieved God knew how, and punishable by Him. 'Mammoth air disaster, five hundred dead . . .' It was asking for trouble. She should refuse to go. Jim would think she was scared, which she was: she also hated the planes themselves, the vulgarity of them, faked up to look like birds. The pipes and rivets and noisy engines.

If she was going to refuse she ought to do it before the luggage went on. He wouldn't go without her, he would follow her home in cold anger. He couldn't keep anything hot for long, it gave him an advantage even when he was in the wrong, whereas she ended up in burnt pieces however quietly and legitimately she had begun.

He had the trolley moving. He said something which she did not hear. She walked away into the crowd. Everyone was making a noise, shouting, talking, laughing, babies and a coloured woman were crying. There wasn't one shut, silent mouth. And tons of luggage were being toted to and fro. And she was being buffeted. She felt and could recognise the buffets of the globular bellies of men and the slabular chests of women. She panicked, nothing now to do with the plane or being airborne. She was being suffocated by people.

She went back to him. He was standing with his hands on the bar

[64]

of the trolley, patient, but ready to inch forward in the queue. His mouth was closed, it had a pursy look nowadays as if he was saving up to speak. He was watching other people's luggage weighed in and there was a nimbus of calm about him. Connie went close. Surrounded by the trolleys, she couldn't be buffeted. And she would watch other people's luggage with a semblance of patience.

'Are you all right?'

It could not have been what he was saving up to say. She cried, 'Oh perfectly!' with a too loud laugh. One or two people, for want of anything else to do, turned and looked at her.

He stooped to exclude them. 'Think of it as an air-bus.'

'What?'

'Just a very ordinary form of travel.'

When they were on the plane he put his hand over hers for the take-off. She said, 'Edith would laugh if she could see me.'

'Why?'

'This is the worst time, isn't it?' The plane shuddered. She felt its conscious effort, for less than a moment it really was like a live thing, a bird, straining to raise itself. 'Going up and coming down is when you're most likely –' she pushed her breath out in a laugh – 'to come down.'

He said sharply, 'I think Edith is a bad influence.'

'Why?'

'She's distracting.'

'What have I got to be distracted from?'

'She confuses you. And not only you. I have felt a certain harassment in her presence.'

'Well I haven't. And she's the only friend I have.'

He blinked at her credulously and more than a little troubled. 'The take-off is accomplished,' he said releasing her hand. 'Now we shall climb gradually and imperceptibly to the flight altitude and maintain it.'

Remembering how she had bitched to Edith about him, she felt guilty. It had not been intended, she had not set out to say any of it.

But she saw now, as she didn't then, that he might prefer to be *mis*understood on the matter they had joked about. He might be as sensitive about it as other men. He might want to be thought immoderate in that respect. Especially by Edith – by Edith he might prefer to be thought positively carnal.

Well, it couldn't be helped. What mattered – and still it couldn't be helped, could it? – was that she didn't know. After thirty years of married life. She looked past him to the window. The window was blank. They were being maintained – his word – by clouds. Steam. The same, if you could believe it, as came off bath-water and hot drinks.

She realised the impossibility of anything. It was quite encouraging, and encouraged her not to try. She lay back in her seat.

'It's really not so bad, is it?' he said.

They had barely checked in at the hotel before he was asking, 'Do you like it?'

'Heavens, yes, it must be costing a fortune.'

'It's pricey, but we can afford it. We may not always.'

She walked out on to the balcony. In these first moments of arrival she couldn't bear to be parted from the sun. Insofar as she had any plan, she planned to lie and melt in it.

'When I shall have retired.' He came to stand beside her. 'We may have to retrench. Make some economies. They will, I trust, be minor ones and we should be able to live in a reasonable degree of comfort. Our way of life need not greatly change.'

'Why talk about that now?'

'It's as well to be prepared.'

'I'm not preparing.' She put her face up to the sun and closed her eyes. Her eyelids turned a beautiful Venetian red.

'We're not wholly dependent on material things for happiness, you and I.' She heard caution in his voice, but, revelling in the colour of her eyelids, she thought that's true. He added, more cheerfully, 'You can see the redoubt from here.'

'The what?'

'The old Grimaldi palace. I've always called it the redoubt.'

'Always? How many times have you been here?'

'Once only. Years ago when I was a schoolboy. Picasso wasn't there then. It's the Musée Grimaldi now.'

'Who did you come with?'

'Waldo, and his mother. We were staying on a farm in the hills.'

Connie said idly, already she felt idle, 'Is that why you wanted to come? To come back?'

'I have no particular feeling about Antibes. We were here only for the day.'

He sounded guarded, he probably thought he had something to guard. There was really no need, not from her. Once she would have been hurt that he should think there was need, but she would not have tried to find out what he was hiding.

'Is there still no news of Waldo?' She had opened her eyes the merest crack and was seeing rainbows through her lashes.

'None.'

'I'm not altogether surprised.'

'Why?'

'That house! I'll never forget it.'

'Neither shall I.'

'Well, there you are then.' But wherever he was, he was not with her. 'I blame his wife – what's her name?'

'Blame?'

'For bead curtains and ball fringes and plastic Alsatians. Even if they were back, which they're not. Yet.'

'Back?'

'In fashion. Oh, they'll get their turn, so she might as well hang on to them, I suppose.'

'I remember the house as their home, a lived-in place, unpretentious and comfortable. I was always welcome there and I had no objections to the décor.'

'If you ask me, he had, and one day he couldn't face the balls and beads.' She was already losing what little hold she had on the subject, but he said, 'I'm not asking you,' with frost in his voice. She had overstepped one of his private marks. It was easily done.

Connie turned to rest her elbows on the balcony rail which was hot and comforting. She thought, here am I, getting comfort out of stone, and at the same moment, looking into the courtyard, she saw a woman. When she remembered later and re-examined the moment, really there hadn't been all that much to see – just a woman crossing the courtyard, carrying a tweed coat. One sleeve trailed on the ground. Connie thought, she won't have needed *that*.

'There isn't a shred of evidence to support your theory. Or any other,' said Jim. 'It's pure conjecture. I have given up conjecture.'

The woman stopped by some flowers growing in a stone jar. So far as Connie could see they were the same canna lilies that were in all the Places Victor Hugos and on every bit of raked gravel that passed for a garden. It made her wonder if the woman could have been abroad before.

'If his reasons for going are good enough for him, they will be good enough for me. I am content to wait and hear what they are.'

'Unless he's dead.' She was sorry as soon as she had said it. He couldn't believe in Waldo dead. It had alarmed her when she realised how unbelievable it was to him. But she was over her alarm and had forgotten his, and her remark had been unthinking. 'I mean, he might have had an accident. Or been murdered.'

'There is no evidence to suggest it.'

The woman in the courtyard did something to one of the lilies, fondled or tweaked it or picked off an insect. She wore a blue sun-dress, her arms and neck were white, so she had not been here long enough to get tanned. She wasn't fat but she certainly wasn't thin, she was about Connie's own size. And about Connie's age. Connie came to some conclusions about the woman in those first moments without being, or knowing that she was being, taken with her.

'I'm not here to look for Waldo.'

Connie opened her eyes, raised her brows without speaking. Of course he was. He hadn't come for a holiday, this place wasn't his style, he disliked heat, he disliked extremes. He had come to look for his friend, who despised him. She had never been able to understand why he couldn't see it.

At lunch-time the woman was at a table outside, under a red and white sunshade. Jim went straight to the dining-room and was shown to a table near the service door.

'Why can't we eat outside?' said Connie. 'It's cool under all that green vine stuff.'

'It's air-conditioned in here.'

'I didn't come all this way to be cooped up indoors.'

The waiter pulled out a chair for her.

'After lunch we'll go into the garden.' He picked up the menu. 'I wonder what their crudities are like. There is a subtle difference between the unprepared and the raw.'

'Are we going to do anything together this holiday?'

'A great deal, I trust.' He was crisp, as if he had been expecting something of the sort.

Connie could not see the woman now that she was sitting down. She went on thinking about her, there wasn't much else to think about. She thought of her as she had been in the courtyard, in her blue dress, lifting a white arm which would have the slight tremor – Connie could only guess it at that distance – of the extra flesh between shoulder and elbow which a woman gets in late middle age. This same woman was now sitting under a sunshade wearing a pink silk shirt, her hair taken up and pinned on top of her head, not Connie's style, not Connie's colouring.

'There's a woman here who looks like me.'

'Indeed?'

'I think you should be prepared. You might think she was me and get into trouble for accosting her.'

He bit on something in his hors d'oeuvres which caused him to wince. 'As like as that? They say everyone has a double. I suppose the extraordinary thing is when two identical people find themselves in the same place at the same time.'

Connie decided to experiment. 'Do you know what I look like?'

'Of course.'

'If you look long enough at a thing you stop seeing it.'

'I haven't stopped seeing you.'

He was smiling his letter-box smile, squared lips and teeth – you wouldn't get a letter past those. 'All right then, shut your eyes and describe me.'

'My dear, we're having lunch.'

'It won't take a minute.'

'But how peculiar it would look, sitting here with my eyes shut.'

She prodded her melon. 'They've put Kirsch in this.'

'The crudities are really rather good. Someone has used imagination in making the dressing.'

'Just suppose you're trying to explain what I'm like to someone who's never seen me.'

He looked about, she thought for inspiration, but it turned out that he was looking for the wine waiter. 'To celebrate our arrival we'll have a bottle of Chablis.'

'So far as you're concerned I'm invisible. I really should take advantage of it.' Connie was relishing the luxury of pushing a point to absurdity. 'Are you sure this is me? I mean, is this your wife with you? It could be someone you picked up off the plane, along with the luggage. Any old woman. I do mean any and I do mean old because a young one would be wasted on you. You just wouldn't notice. I don't believe you'd even notice the sex. Any old *person* will do.' She giggled, imagining him taking by the hand some ancient Brownie in a unisex suit.

He had located the wine waiter and gave his order. When the man went he bowed his head over his plate. 'You're five feet four inches tall, weigh about 130 pounds, fair hair, greying, worn in what I

[70]

believe is known as a bouffant style, you have a pink complexion, blue eyes, a small nose, a series of moles along the jaw-bone and at the left temple –'

'Grave-marks!'

'Moles. I distinctly recall wondering, when first we met, if there were others.' Another man, any other man, would have looked at her then, and made it right. He kept his head down. 'Shall I go on?'

'Can you? Oh heavens, it was a joke – I didn't ask for an inventory!'

'I thought you did.'

He was cold with his anger, she was warm, getting hot with hers. 'You didn't prove anything. Where am *I* among all those moles!'

Their wine was brought and he went through the ritual of smelling and tasting and approving. As he filled her glass he said, 'I trust this will be a successful holiday.'

'We must hope you find Waldo, mustn't we?'

They gazed at each other. The creases from his nose to his mouth – how would she describe them? His helplessness transmitted itself to her.

After lunch the hotel garden was invaded by children whose parents were taking the siesta. Children pounded between the flowerbeds, exploding the gravel underfoot, their cries rocketing, and Connie suggested that since she didn't feel any need to sleep and it would be impossible to rest in the garden, they go to look at the sea.

'The Med.' She understood it was tideless, but that hadn't stopped it from leaving a tide mark, a soupy rim where on occasions it crept up the beach, not in white skeins like the English Channel, but sneaking up to deposit some of its plastic bottles and broken snorkels. All the same, its presence made physically, socially and morally acceptable the long glutinous hours she would spend splayed out on the beach. 'It has its uses.' She meant that to lie in the sun without any sea to hand would be squalid. Like people who sat in bathing-suits in their back gardens and on London rooftops.

Jim put on his sun-glasses. Then he looked like a spy. No one who only saw him in them could know how he was to be trusted. 'Perhaps we could go the Place Fontaine.'

'What's there?'

'The car-hire people. I ought to see about getting something as soon as possible. Having a car will make all the difference. We can drive to Grasse and along the Corniche. And I should like to see the Grand Canyon. There is one, you know, not as big as in America, but still very impressive.'

She didn't know and she had a feeling of the multiplicity of things which had recently started to come: a part of ageing, she supposed. It could not be said to be an increase in knowing, it was a realisation of unknowing. 'What about Disneyland? And Big Ben? Have they got those here too?' He might have said yes, without surprising her. But he lowered his chin and looked at her over his dark lenses and she cried fretfully, 'Why is everything so mixed up nowadays?'

'I think you'll like to see the perfumeries. Grasse is no distance, barely fifteen miles away.'

'I shall like it if we go together.'

'Of course.' He amended, 'Of course we shall go together,' fearing, as well she knew, that she might think that he considered his presence a guarantee of satisfaction. 'The Mediterranean separates Europe, Africa and Asia. That is quite a function.'

'And it's nice to be beside it.'

'You know,' he took off his glasses, 'polarisation rather enhances the effect of the light on the water.'

It was when they were looking at the Picasso drawings in the Chateau museum that she knew she had definite hopes of the holiday. And of everything else. Those ridiculous pictures reassured her. They were scribbles really, and comic. Obviously they weren't meant to be taken seriously. She paused before one of a creature with dog's ears swallowing a pair of knitting-needles, and a female rising out of a sea of kisses. The female, which was more of a formula than a form, had a pin head, arms like bolsters and round, astonished breasts.

'They're single-line drawings. Apparently that's tremendous. Tremendous simplicity.' Jim had got a book from somewhere and read out the title of the drawing: ' "Faune jouant de la Diaule et Centaure au Trident devant la Femme Fleur".'

'I suppose it's sexy.' Connie giggled. 'I can't make out the anatomy of the man showing off his one big underarm hair.'

'The man is half horse, that's the horse's foreleg. There's the hoof.' Jim lowered his eyes to the page. 'It says here that the spirit of the drawings is innocent and joyful. Picasso was in his sixties when he did this.'

'Old enough to know better – better, I mean, than anyone else.' Because, she thought, these were private doodles she was looking at, and they carried a message which she was glad to get. Things could be boiled down, made tenable, they could even be made funny: that was the message.

' "His talents are essentially linear, the more you look, the more you will discover." ' Jim raised his eyes. 'Presumably that is where the artistry comes in.'

She had no intention of looking for more. It would be like working back to what had been joyfully abandoned. 'Oh I'm sure there's more!' and it would have been more than *she* was up against, she was thinking.

'You like Picasso?'

'He's been a great help.'

'Then shall we go and see about the car?'

'Of course – the car.'

'One never knows, there may be difficulties.'

'What difficulties?'

'I'd like to get it settled.' He compressed his lips. He had random veins of obstinacy, but this one was traceable from start to finish.

They walked to the Place Fontaine and she said she would rather not go inside but would wait in the sun. He left her, purposefully crossed the street, wearing his purpose like an overcoat. Did he think it didn't show? More to the point, and no need to ask, he didn't care that it showed. He was going to get a car and drive around looking for Waldo Klein. She felt exasperation and some pity. She would feel more if he found Waldo. For one thing, she didn't like the man: for another, this was Jim's chance to get clear. Or was it? Was there another chance that Waldo's ghost would prove as strong, or stronger, than his flesh and blood?

A voice said, 'Where now?' and another answered, 'Hotel Candide, over there where the old guy's going.' Jim had paused in a doorway on the far side of the Place to look back at her, and two young men with tender necks and baseball thighs were at her elbow. One of them smiled at her through wire spectacles. Then they moved away across the square.

Old. That too. It wasn't the very first time she had faced up to the word. For both of them. It meant that there was no hope of a change: old dog can't be taught new tricks, old wine mustn't go into new bottles, no fool like an old fool. Yet here she was, apparently still hoping. She had armed herself with the sun and was full of hope.

She hurried after the young men. She was going to stand beside Jim, not saying anything, not to them, but letting them know all the same that she knew what they thought and that it didn't matter. To her, or to him. She would let them see that she and Jim had reached an undercutting time of life and had lived through a lot to get to it. It undercut anything they might think. She went into the car-hire office which was full of people talking about cars. The young men were not there.

Jim, waiting his turn, looked questioningly at her and she said, 'I came in to get out of the sun.'

V

Jessel was looking towards the redoubt from their balcony. He had hardly been alone for more than a few moments since they arrived two days ago. Of course he was glad to have Connie's company, he was grateful for it. But there would be occasions when her presence here would be uncontemporaneous because she had simply not been where he had been at a material time. For all he knew of her at that time, she had not been anywhere.

He would have preferred that she understood the situation even if she could not appreciate it. The idea of trying to convey it was daunting. How, for instance, could he tell her what he was thinking at this moment? He was not actually thinking. He was dipping, dabbling in the past. Mooning. Memories, at this distance of time, were unreliable. It was a weakness, and unfaithfulness of a kind, to do what he was doing. And entirely without profit. Yet if his course of action were to be examined it would be obvious that he had come resolved to moon.

This evening the sea was a luminous pearl. Ships slipping past dissolved like sugar into the pink haze round the Cap.

The day they had come to Antibes Mrs Klein had been in a mood. She seemed to be hearing, against her will, an interior monologue, as if someone, not altogether herself, was telling her unsettling things. She sat on the train, stirring more than was necessary, more than the motion of the carriage required, smiling brilliantly when she met his eyes and just as brilliantly when she did not. Her smile was like a mirror, impossible to see what lay behind it.

They reached Antibes and were walking round the ramparts when Jessel paused to watch an artist at work. She and Waldo sauntered on, she trailing her parasol behind her.

'Any good?' said Waldo when Jessel caught up with them.

'Not bad.'

'Don't ask me to go to any exhibitions. Looking at pictures bores me to tears.' She lifted her shoulders and arms in an elaborated shrug. 'I never can see beyond the brushmarks. I don't know a Van Gogh –' she pronounced it Van Go – 'from a Renault.'

'A Renault's a car, Bunny dear,' said Waldo.

'That's what I mean.'

'Renoir,' said Jessel.

Waldo lost his temper and shouted at her. 'Don't pretend! Who the devil are you pretending for?'

'It might just be natural, don't you think?'

Waldo seized her arm and pulled her round to face him. 'I won't have you making a fool of yourself.'

She touched his cheek. 'I do it for your sake, not mine.'

It had not been a happy day. She and Waldo had private sources of mirth which they shared; Jessel could not join in, he never knew what they were laughing about and feared that in his ignorance he would contribute to their amusement. Their laughter would stop as suddenly as it had begun and she would turn on the mirror smile which was her way of showing absence of pleasure.

Jessel would never forget the motion of her body as she walked. Each movement was part of a small but perfect cycle, starting from the moment when she was aligned and poised, a complete, beautifully executed woman in a dazzling white dress, with a parasol which, opened and laid on her shoulder, slightly dimmed the brightness of her hair and skin. But nothing, nothing stopped the actual performance which was what he, after the first demonstration, or even before, was waiting for. There occurred each time the exact same degree of fall and rise, left hip and right. He had had a mercifully incomplete vision of her without clothes and without flesh, the big ballbones rolling silkily in their sockets.

Connie came and stood beside him on the balcony. She was damp from her bath and wore only a petticoat. Hot water and emotion transformed Connie. They took years off her, when she was angry and after a bath she looked like a girl.

'What are you thinking about?'

'I'm watching the sunset. It does seem a relatively quicker business here. Quicker than at home.'

'I shall stay on the beach tomorrow. All day.'

'You'll get burnt.'

'I'll have a beach umbrella and oil myself and fry a gentle golden brown.' He managed to avoid wincing. But they had been married for more than thirty years and he had to allow for her working knowledge; she knew that he found the prospect distasteful. 'What will you do?'

'I'll come to the beach with you.'

'This is my holiday too. I want to enjoy myself and I can't do that while you're in a state of abject misery beside me. As you were today.'

'I suffered some physical discomfort. But you said you wanted us to be together.'

'Not at the price of your martyrdom.'

It had certainly cost him something. The beach had been a hell. The light, which was clinical without being the least antiseptic, had got behind his sunglasses and behind his eyes, so that he was dazzled internally. In addition there was the noise, piercing cries as barbaric and shrill as the screams of creatures in the jungle, the roar of speedboats, the whistle of jets – all brought into his eardrums by the weight, the sheer barometric pressure of the air.

He said, 'This is the south of France, there are no martyrs here.'

'You once told me that the south of France was all extremes.'

'Did I?' In a rough and ready way it expressed what he felt. He loved and hated the place. 'A sweeping statement. But when I came here I was at an age when everything is extreme. Very young people don't allow for mediums.' Certainly not happy ones, certainly he had not realised that it was possible, and preferable, to be moderately happy. 'When shall we go to Grasse?'

[77]

'The next day or the day after that. While I'm doing what I like and you don't, you must do exactly what *you* like. It's only fair.'

And she would be fairly content. He hoped that it would be enough, that she would have a sufficiency of happy memories to take back. It was up to him to see that she had. 'Very well. I'll go for a drive.'

As they sat at dinner he identified the woman whom she thought resembled her. The likeness, in his opinion, was superficial and had to be sought. The woman's features were Connie's style, but she showed her bones where Connie did not. Connie had always had a pleasing roundness, to which she had added over the years: her cheeks, her chin, her bosom and the cushions of her fingers were now a little rounder, a little less soft than formerly. The woman was younger and more stylish than Connie. He did not himself find stylishness desirable. He wondered if Connie wanted it, believed that she had it?

'Where will you go for your drive?'

'Into the hills. I want to get out and walk.'

'Where will you walk?'

'There are paths.' He remembered old limestone blocks worn away and chipped, ascending in shallow steps through ragwort and flowering broom and blue daisies and giant convolvulus. 'It's not so long since mules were the only form of transport in the hills and the old tracks still exist.'

'How quaint.'

She had taken to drinking down her wine as soon as her glass was filled. He poured some iced water. This she ignored. 'By the by,' he said, 'I think I've seen your double.'

'My what?'

'The woman you said looks like you.'

'Oh, that woman.'

'She's sitting at the table by the pillar. Wearing a green dress.' Connie turned and stared. The younger woman raised her head and stared back. 'I see what you mean,' he said. 'But of course I wouldn't mistake her for you.'

Connie had a knack of emptying her face not only of the thoughts she had on the matter under discussion, but on any matter whatsoever. When it happened he neither knew the cause nor how to deal with the effect, except by wiping out his own thoughts. Certainly by keeping them to himself.

The next morning he drove carefully. The hired car was unfamiliar, a smaller, lighter vehicle than he was used to and he felt vulnerable. He ventured on the autoroute and immediately found himself in several minds as to which lane he ought to take. It was cut and thrust in every one, as far as he could see there was no differentiation by speed. Since he was unsure of his turn off, or of what the car was capable, he decided to stay in a middle lane and hold a steady fifty miles an hour.

'Hold' was the operative word. The engine was over-eager, the little light chassis threatened to bounce or be bounced off the road. He gripped the wheel and stooped – he felt he was in an abnormally confined space – to stare through the windscreen. A camion, beating past, missed him by a hair's breadth.

'Priorité à droite!' He usually forebore talking to himself, but on the road one was, whatever the chances of being heard, addressing other road-users. Something came alongside, an engine-cab, rip-roaring and with its entire traction system exposed. Being a Continental vehicle the driver was able to look directly upon him. Jessel glimpsed an elbow propped on the wound-down window, a grubby canvas cap tipped over the man's face. It was all he had time for. The cab was pulling a train of open-sided cages containing animals. The cages drew level on his nearside, so close that he cried out in alarm.

He tried to escape into the next lane. At once klaxons blared hysterically from the following traffic. The cages followed him. He glimpsed the word 'Circus' painted on a tarpaulin broken loose and thrashing in the wind. He slowed down. Again there was a cacophony from behind. The cages had come so close that he saw, with the scrupulosity of panic, hairs clotted on the bars. He looked into the eyes of a huge, maned lion. It was crouched as if to spring, snarling with yellow teeth and wet red jaws only inches away.

The moment was nearly his last: he could have died and so might others, not in the jaws of the lion but in a tangle of crashed cars. Somehow he held to his course, neither slowed nor accelerated nor swerved. He grasped the wheel and waited for death. And the cages drew past, inch by inch. The lions, tigers and chimpanzees looked in at him with hatred, indifference and sadness. The tarpaulin flew like a banner over the retreating vans.

He drove off at the next exit. It was an underpass and took him into a vast car-park. He drew into the first free space. He was sweating, something he rarely did, and his hands were fused to the steering-wheel – hands which had done and knew how to do a lot of things, which because of age were now inclined unnecessarily to re-do some things, to fidget, over-confirm. How much trust could he put in them? He had no choice but to put it all. The fact that they had just held his life was not encouraging for he had at no time been certain they could give it back.

What was left of it. In a few years, six to be exact, he would have reached three-score and ten, the generally accepted life-quota, after which anything more was regarded as borrowed time. People did not say, 'Goodness, how sad,' when a person of seventy-plus died. They said, 'He's had his life.'

He loosed his fingers from the wheel. They came off white and shrivelled. He snapped them to restore the circulation. Young women in suntops and bikinis were pushing trolleys laden with groceries across the park, coming, he surmised, from the hypermarket on the Cap. He watched them without lubricity. They were right, in their impropriety they were proper. All that firm brown flesh was not merely desirable, it was essential, the desire was essential. But he was expendable.

It should make him carefree rather than careful. He leaned over and wound down the far window. The smell of diesel oil and frying crêpes came into the car and filled him with a sort of inorganic hunger. That, and the young women whom he did not covet but who were in God's good time. He could, he did, admire and cherish them. Everything under the sun remained to be enjoyed. If all he was short of was time, he must hang on to his entitlement. And if time was not all he was short of, six years might yet be enough, might have been meted out for him.

He got out of the car and followed the people going into the hypermarket. It was an astonishing place, with fountains and statuary, a swimming-pool, cafés, restaurants, rondpoints, galleries, gardens, play areas and shops to cater for every taste, except for the poorly-paid. He drank coffee at a brasserie and bought chocolate for Connie from a Japanese girl who placed her palms together as if for prayer and bowed to him.

He had no intention of returning to the autoroute. His fear was still in the car. It was all there in the heat which had built up while the car was stationary. The steering-wheel burned his hands, the seat burned his body from buttocks to shoulders. The instruments on the dials glowed yellow. He had inadvertently switched on the panel light.

He rolled down the windows, started the engine and the cooler-fan and drove into the underpass. All that heat and he still had a nut of cold inside him. The cold was a chemical cold. He knew that on the return journey he would have to drive at least twenty kilometres on the autoroute to melt the nut.

The underpass took him into steep streets which must once have gone right down to the beach before they were cut short by the autoroutes. He would remember them for the preponderantly Victorian-Raj style of the buildings. Some of the villas looked like stone howdahs. The streets were packed with frenetic drivers and even more frenetic pedestrians. There was a gaiety about the enormities they committed and the risks they took. It was rather like driving through a carnival.

Outside the town he was on a D-road which angled and doubled on itself, climbing to the foothills of the maritime range. Signposts promised places which were only names on the map to him. If he was planning to go to La Bigorne he would need to make a sharp turn south. It was possible that the holiday would slip by without his having been anywhere near it. One should not return with expectations, and he was full of them. They had not been realised fifty years ago and certainly wouldn't be now. Why did Connie think he meant to go to La Bigorne? Because she thought he meant to look for Waldo there. He sighed, lifted the tips of his fingers from the wheel and dropped them. It was increasingly difficult to know why Connie thought anything.

He was finding the standard of driving in France reprehensible. The most fundamental safety procedures were ignored, were flouted with verve and precision. He had to allow the precision. It seemed to be a matter of principle to break the rules of the road. Of course the French were individualists, and when in France so were the Germans, Italians and Americans. The British roistered on their wheels. Every GB car, burdened though it might be with luggage, children and grandparents, pursued him up hill and down until it could pass at the most inauspicious, not to say dangerous, moment.

He was not travelling through an area of outstanding natural beauty and although he kept his attention on the road he was satisfied that he was missing little in the way of scenery. His nose rather than his eyes informed him as he passed into a 'Domaine de Fragrance'. It was a huge nursery with acres of glass-houses. The air smelt of the stuff they used to spray cinema-foyers with when he was a boy. The idea then had been to charm and hypersensitise the patrons as they went in with something Eastern and musky. Waldo used to hold his nose, but Jessel had liked it. It predisposed him to things which he normally fought shy of. It was the nearest he came to being seduced in those days.

The road took him into a cleft in the hills. As yet they were mere swellings, but on a spur of rock he glimpsed an old fortified town. 'Ville pittoresque', declared the road-signs. 'Visitez sa citadelle, ses grottes, sa cascade, son jardin d'acclimatation, ses belles terrasses,

ses restaurants provençaux. Bienvenu!' Fifty years ago he had come to Antibes by train. It was a lifetime. The Chairman of the board of his company, one of the dozen most influential men in the country, was still waiting in the womb fifty years ago. Yet Jessel remembered that day in Antibes – spent in the absence of his Chairman and other unborn millions, and in the lifetimes of millions now dead – more pressingly than he remembered the events of yesterday. It had been an infinitely memorable day, infinity being as long as he himself should live. He had a perfect vision of the train, its toy-bright coaches and an engine gold-banded like a cigar, sniffing its way through the hills, delicately inhaling through its smoke-stack and emitting contralto shrieks in the rocky defiles. The driver did it to make echoes for the amusement of the passengers, Waldo said. The French didn't miss a trick, Waldo said, look how they had yanked out olive groves to open up the view. There was more money in tourists than olives. Mrs Klein had turned to Jessel and her eyes looked into his. She had dark eyes, between black and brown, wonderfully lustrous. 'In the old days,' she said, 'the Ligne du Sud was a romantic little railway. The scenery was just so much heartache. Torn from the arms of her beloved, what did a woman care for ravines and waterfalls and ruined chateaux? I wonder how many Edwardian ladies have wept beneath their veils as they were rushed back to their husbands in Cannes or Nice – perhaps in this very carriage.' Jessel was wondering how a human eye, which he understood was an arrangement of jelly and nerves for the purposes of seeing, could be at once brilliant and plush and at once swallow him whole and reduce his image to the size of a fraction of a tealeaf. 'My mother was one of the ladies who wept.' She was, as so often, talking intimately to him. She placed her gloved hand, not on his knee which he could not have borne, but on the seat beside him. 'How she must have hated these glimpses of the sea!'

'You were in Austria, Mouse,' said Waldo. 'How would you know what went on?'

Mrs Klein was not wearing a veil. She had on a charming little hat

[83]

with a feather curled under the brim. The low cut neck of her dress was filled with a delicate lace which concealed nothing. Jessel dared not look. In the early morning, when she had first appeared ready for the journey he had seen the inalienable shadow between her breasts. He had the vision in his head. And it was the mention of her mother, whom he immediately translated to Mrs Klein herself – hat, dress, gloves, shadow and all – which had immeasurably extended the day in time. He could and did believe that she had a lover and that it was she who could not bear the sight of the sea. When at last she lowered her lashes and sighed, but did not weep, he thought it was because it was a moment too soon for her tears. In a rage, he had risen from his seat and joined Waldo who was leaning out of the carriage window. 'My grandmama never sowed a wild oat in her life,' said Waldo. Jessel said, 'It's all the same to me.' Waldo hung from his waist out of the window and tore a clump of grass from the bank, 'It had better be, because her daughter's a bloody liar.'

A young man riding a motorbike somewhere just above the level of the road jumped his machine down and landed a few yards ahead of Jessel. He did a right-about roar and was off in the opposite direction while Jessel was still treading on his brakes. He was naked except for a pair of tattered briefs of the same poignant blue as the Crau men's trousers, but Jessel was brought back to a point slightly prior to the fellow's criminal irresponsibility and much later than those other memories. He realised what it was while the car tyres still squealed. In Antibes he had seen the same young man, bearded face, corkscrew curls, slender ribcage and all, hanging in a church with a nail driven through his insteps. Here he was now, or had been, lacking only his cross and crown of thorns, stunting on a motorbike.

The road started to climb in earnest. Jessel changed down, and down again. Below what he hoped was a hard shoulder the ground dropped precipitately into a forested valley. He was looking down on to the tops of the trees. There were olive-groves on the slopes above him. Had they always been so tidy? The terraces, fronted with cream-coloured boulders, rose like an amphitheatre up the hillside.

Soon he was stooping over his knees, scrambling up the steep slope. He came to a building site which was deserted. It was past twelve o'clock, the southern lunch-break had begun. Three new villas, as yet only shells of breeze and timber, were wedged against the hill at strategic points. Open-fronted, agape, each had appropriated a vista across forests and hills to the sea, each looked like a chicken-coop. Jessel picked his way past concrete-mixers. He smelt new wood and the old inimical whiff of wet stone. There were empty Gauloise packets and bottles which had held Pilsner and Vin de Maurin. Half-buried in builder's sand was a pair of woman's corsets, complete with laces. He touched them curiously with his foot. He did not begrudge enjoyments which were remote from his own.

Beyond the site the track dwindled to a defile between rocks. He walked with cushions of scabious and umbrellas of wild parsley growing above his head, and then the rock wall plunged away down the hillside, leaving him poised on a narrow step of earth held together by roots of grass and thorn. The bastions of limestone were piled on top of one another like huge cheeses. And if the sound of the cigales had become a cliché, it was no less meaningful. The vibration of the insects' legs produced in him an almost intolerable dismay. Whatever he had lost, it had been through every fault of his own. And wasn't he harbouring some damned silly idea – of a silliness which damned at the outset – of becoming reconciled to it? He hurried along the path, not caring how he stumbled on the uneven ground and once, when his shoe caught in a root, was thrown on his hands and knees. Then he realised that he was doing another damned silly thing: he was trying to get away from the cigales.

After that he put his hands in his pockets and made himself stroll and look up at the moon-country. Rounding a bend of the path he came upon a ruin. It was very old, a church or an abbey, built into an outcropping of the rock. It occupied several levels. The first was below that of the path, and what remained of the walls – or perhaps the cloisters – hid his view of the nave. There were arches, broken at different points so that it was possible to guess at the complete structure. They must have sprung one from the other, spanning the face of the rock. The stone was very dark. He remembered an ominous phrase: time will darken it, and was suddenly conscious of the coolness. Where the hills pulsed out heat, this place had a cold breath. He was made very much aware of the difference in temperature, for while his right side was still in sun, his left, and his head, were in shadow. He recalled the hostile smell of wet stone on the building site. That same smell was sublimated here, by the architecture of course, the springing arches and the built-to-last – and still lasting – columns.

He had no fixed intention to explore, but as it was here and was throwing light on his state of mind and might throw more – less inept, he hoped – he scrambled down from the path. When he stood on the rock on which the place was built, he was completely in shadow. And now the chill and the smell combined to make something else, an affirmation and a celebration. Yes, he thought, someone once had gloried in the shortevity of the flesh. Perhaps it was the right thing to do. It was certainly the dignified thing to do.

He walked into a porchway, four massive columns broken off, some high, some to their base, as if by bungling blows or varying frenzies. Beyond lay what was in effect a walled garden. Except that no one had planted or ever tended it. Plants that hung on in the blistering heat outside were privileged and even pampered here: fig, blackberry, broom, blue thistles and white convolvulus and great tilting agaves with leaves like broadswords. Another sort of congregation, he thought, and whoever built this place, if he could see it now, would think it a step in the right direction.

He felt no incentive to push into the mass of vegetation and was turning to go when he saw someone in the shadow. At first he thought it was a boy, a young boy of nine or ten. He was startled, had the guilty feeling that his thoughts were watched. Then the figure stepped into the light and he saw that it was female. There was no doubt when she moved. Her movements had the grace and angularity of a Balinese dancer. She was dressed in jeans and T-shirt and her hair was cropped to a bristle all over her head.

'Hi.'

He said, 'Bonjour.'

'I thought you were a ghost.'

'I beg your pardon?'

'Because of the way you were creeping about.'

'I was not creeping.'

'You were and so was I. I thought *I* was a ghost. It's foul in here, isn't it?'

He didn't feel disposed either to agree or to question her and was moving away with a nod which was surely all that was necessary after so brief an encounter. She said, 'It was holy, this place. Sacred to something.'

He couldn't resist saying, 'To the death of mankind.'

'It's fun cocking snooks, but you must stop somewhere or the cocking becomes pointless. You must leave a few snooks, and God's the biggest.'

He distrusted people who introduced weighty considerations into the first moments of an encounter. But probably he had brought it on himself. He put back a bramble with the toe of his shoe. 'I like it as it is.' He would be glad to get out of the place. Liking was not what he felt. He felt that he had had thrust on him something arbitrary and untenable to be going on with. And whether he went on with it or not, he would be left with the suspicion. He scrambled back on to the path and stood easing his bones into the warmth of the sun.

The girl appeared between the columns of the porch. 'Where are you going?'

'Up into the hills.'

'I shouldn't if I were you.'

'Why not?'

'There's going to be a storm.'

He looked up at the sky. The sun still rode overhead, but from

[88]

behind the mountains a continent of cloud approached. Indigo caverns opened and closed, they exerted a diminishing effect on the eye, like a convex mirror. Within their depths the lightning was no bigger than a nerve. The girl said, 'I was in these hills once when there was a storm and the rain went up my nose, I couldn't breathe. You'll get soaked all right.' She sounded reassuring, as if he might be worrying that he wouldn't. 'I'm going to run for the village.'

She had a canvas shoulder-bag which she tossed on to the path and sprang after it, spreading her arms like wings. They did indeed seem to raise her. He watched the curiously disassociated joy in her movements. She was not, he thought, as aware of it as her body was: that was one of the fringe benefits of youth appreciated only in old age.

He looked again at the sky. In a very short while the sun would be blotted out and if he wished to know what it would be like he had only to look at the moon-country where the limestone bastions were moving under a solid curtain of rain.

There was no point in getting wet, it might be worse than pointless. He had a tendency to arthritic bouts which he was having increasing difficulty in keeping to himself. Drying out in the sun, supposing there was any more sun that day, would be inviting trouble. He was not happy, either, about being shut in the car during an electric storm. In these mountains the weather had every appearance of going to extremes. Furthermore, it was almost one o'clock and if he got something to eat in the village he might walk on when the storm had passed.

The girl was not in sight, but there were so many twists and turns in the path that she need not have been far ahead. He thought perhaps she had flown down from the rock on those slender arms of hers, bending them at the elbow and turning her fingers to catch the currents of air. The first drop of rain struck him on the nose. He looked up. The sky above his head was radiant and unclouded. To his left the fringe of the cloud mass was the colour of gall. He began to run. The rain took pot-shots, hitting him in singular places – on the ear, the back of the neck, in the parting of his hair. It rapidly ceased to discriminate and scored all over him. He reached the road with his shirt clinging to his shoulders.

The café on the corner had a terrasse raised above the street and covered with a crimson and white awning. The tables were all occupied by people taking shelter.

He went inside to a room which smelt of food, Gauloises, garlic and coffee. There was one vacant table facing a door marked WC. The room was dark and darkening as the storm developed. The light bulbs, of low wattage and sparse, barely pricked the gloom. There was a counter at one end and around that and the pinball tables were the men who had been rained off their game of boules, workers from the building site, and local barflies. Tourists and holiday-makers had settled for lunch at the tables. The patron behind the bar was smoking a cheroot, his wife and daughter and a hunchback boy were serving the tables. It was noisy and hot. Jessel looked out of the window. The rain had arrived and was drowning out every sign of life and movement except its own. The element of air was gone. The village square held the water like a glass. The canvas awning outside the café was filling so fast that it sagged on to the heads of the people underneath. Young men in leather shorts leaped up to punch the bulge.

The hunchback came to Jessel and handed him a smudged sheet handwritten in purple ink. Jessel ordered without consulting it. He disliked omelettes but it was impossible to decipher the menu and he couldn't think of anything else to ask for.

'Au fromage?' said the hunchback. 'Champignons? Nature?'

On the last word came the loudest clap of thunder Jessel had ever heard. He quite thought they were being bombed. He thought he was having his last moment, that for him and everything within radius this was the process of being annihilated. He judged, afterwards, that in the moment which followed, the café and indeed the whole village could never have been so still since they were built. The hunchback gazed at him white-eyed. He was little more than a child and had nowhere else to turn. His irreconcilable smithereens hung with Jessel's in the air.

But he recovered first. Grimacing and gesturing upwards with his thumb he declared, 'Nature!' Then everyone went on with whatever they had been doing, or started something noisier. The girl Jessel had seen at the ruin came in from the terrasse. She passed him with a nod and went into the WC. Men revenged themselves, kicking and thumping. The patron shouted and the hunchback was hoisted on to one of the pinball tables. He tucked in his elbows and bent his knees threatening to jump through the glass. The blackish humour was solid enough to cut with a knife.

The girl came back through the door of the WC and stopped by Jessel's table. Her T-shirt clung to her like a skin, cotton-sculpted over her small breasts. 'Someone emptied the awning on me.'

'How unfortunate.'

'The street's foaming. It's the sort of rain that goes up as well as down. Come and look.'

'Thank you, no. I'm going to have some lunch. Shouldn't you do something about your wet clothes?'

'I can't take them off.' Smiling, she pinched up a fold of the T-shirt from between her breasts. 'Nothing underneath.'

'Will you join me for lunch?' He was immediately outraged at himself. He not only had no intention of saying it, had not wished or remotely thought of saying it, but he had sounded like a radio comic as he said it.

'I don't want to eat. I'll have a coffee.' She sat down in the chair facing him. There was rain in her hair, in the stubble, and he caught the smell of her flesh warming her wet clothes. She was probably steaming slightly; he did not see it because of the smoky atmosphere. 'I'm waiting for the bus.'

'Which bus?'

'The two o'clock.' He looked at his watch. It wanted a quarter to the hour. She was smiling and he thought how odd it was, and delusory, that the one movement of lips could have so many different interpretations. He could perfectly interpret hers. She still had the fold of wet T-shirt in her fingertips and she had, as near as made no matter, forgotten it. It was not expected to matter to him. 'Your omelette looks awful. Are you going to eat it?'

He took a mouthful and swallowing in haste, almost choked. Between coughs he asked again, 'Which bus – where to?'

'Grivedoré.'

'Is that far?'

Her smile vanished. 'Far enough.'

He found that he could not imagine and would not wish to have her smiling. The cropped hair, one of those well-nigh offensive styles which young people adopted, was right for her. It was a setting which displayed, actually proffered, the disposition of her features. Nose, mouth, brows, would have been ordinarily pretty in a frame of long hair. It also declared her youth – which was not in doubt – and qualities like candour, courage and innocence, which could be. There was a pause. She gazed at him, he thought she was trying to keep something in check. 'Where is Grivedoré?'

Whatever it was could not be checked by looking at him, and she moved in her chair, first one way, then the other. 'Isn't it foul here!'

It was the second time she had used the word in their brief acquaintance. He supposed it came naturally and was glad, as always, that he and Connie had no children. He would not have known how to cope with their arbitrary and wholesale disapproval.

'Here's your coffee. You had better drink it at once.' She obeyed, and as she swallowed kept her eyes on his face with something which was curiosity or trust, he couldn't be sure which. 'I wouldn't choose to eat here –' he pushed away the omelette, the radio had been switched on and a huge, disciplined bleating climbed on top of the existing noise, even the thunder was incorporated – 'but it will serve to ride out the storm.'

She said something which he could not hear. The radio was being blasted by atmospheric interference. Someone, liking it, turned up the volume. She was looking at the omelette, he thought he caught the word 'religion' but she was making no special effort to be heard. He made none to hear. He sat and watched her. He did not often have the time or wish to study a face as supremely young as hers. The supremacy was not directed against him: he felt it, she had it. At the same time he felt a wry sympathy because for her everything was to be done from the beginning. His heart failed him, or perhaps it was his stomach recoiling.

He caught the word 'Christianity'. And then she said, through a hole in the noise, 'It's stick and carrot.'

'I beg your pardon?'

'Catholicism, Buddhism, Mohammedism, Salvation Armyism, they're names for the same old thing, reward and punishment. It makes sense, with our record.' She was looking at his omelette. 'I'm hungry but I've still got a few hang-ups.'

'It isn't very nice, let me order you something else –'

'I shan't eat until it's over. I shan't do anything till it's over.'

'I'm afraid I don't follow.'

'As a mark of respect.' She opened her eyes wide, it might have been daring or provocative but there was a touch of panic, too. 'Why I'm going to Grivedoré – a friend of mine died and I have to scatter his ashes in the lake. What do they call it?'

'A committal. I'm sorry.'

'We used to go there for our holidays. We had a hut on the lakeside, Maurice said it was out of this world. So's he now, he was always dying.' She sounded brisk and factual and Jessel wondered what she meant by respect, whether it transcended conventional attitudes towards the dead, or exploded them. 'He had multiple sclerosis so there was plenty of time. We pretended we were going to live by the lake for the rest of our lives. We pretended we'd get old. He was going to catch fish and we'd eat figs and peaches in summer and berries in winter. We didn't want to think about money because we didn't have any and I suppose because money's real and we couldn't be. We used to quarrel a lot. We couldn't agree even about how many cooking pots we'd need. We'd spend a whole afternoon

[93]

deciding whether you can fry eggs in a saucepan.' She leaned over and pushed up Jessel's cuff to look at his watch. 'The bus is due. It's stopped raining, I'll go outside and wait.' Her fingers rested a moment on his wrist. 'I've not told anyone about Maurice.'

He was left considering whether it meant that he was the only person she had told, or that she regarded him as no one. Conversely, he was free to suppose that she rated him as some one deserving of her confidence.

He watched long after she had gone out of the café and out of sight. He could still see a detail of her, the decorative way she held her arms, angled from the elbows. Outside, the daylight was spiked by the sun flashing on storm water.

VI

'I see what you mean.'

Seeing what he meant her to mean, Connie could have laughed out loud. She wanted it to be known that she was laughing, that she could laugh. She was feeling the slight unhingement and the heightened sensibility she always felt after drinking wine. Not that it took much sensibility to guess what he was thinking. The woman in the green dress whom he thought, or was pretending to think, looked like her, was pretty and smart and knew how to wear her clothes. Also she was at least twenty-five years younger. And she wasn't in the least like Connie or like Connie had been, so just what had he seen when he looked thirty years ago?

'But I don't think I should ever mistake her for you.' He was studying the menu. 'What do you think? Fish or fowl? I don't trust beef on the Continent, and the veal can be insipid. There's baron of hare, fricassée of rabbit, Ceylon curry, chicken à la Marengo, duck with pineapple and something called Suffolk ham which is hardly likely.'

'Why?'

'In the Baie des Anges?'

'If you don't like the food and you don't like the sun, why did we come? Why didn't we go to Bournemouth?'

'If you had expressed any preference, we would have. I don't dislike the food and I thought you liked the sun.'

'So we're here for my sake?' She was smiling and if he had looked at her he would have seen that she was ready to be grateful. He concentrated on crumbling his bread. 'I suppose you'll go to that place where you stayed – what's it called?' She had been supposing it since he told her that he had been there with Waldo: of course it was

[95]

his reason for coming to Antibes. The holiday was an excuse and her happening to like the sun was his luck.

'La Bigorne.'

He was on guard, the same guard of the same something. And whatever he was guarding had to do with Waldo Klein. Perhaps with Daisy? Had he promised Daisy to do what he could to find Waldo?' And all that he could think of was to go back to a place where they had once been together – as if he was on a pilgrimage?

'You think you'll find him at this Bighorn place.' He shook his head. She cried, 'You think he's gone back to the scene of his childhood. Let me tell you it's most unlikely and I'm surprised at you.' Actually she wasn't. It was the sort of sentimental notion men cherished, and might act on, and he wasn't as free of sentiment as he liked to make out. But Waldo was. 'Waldo wouldn't go back there in a million years.'

'No.'

'You will, you'll go back for old times' sake.' The truth of the matter was he wanted to be alone with his memories. She knew that he had quite a thing about Waldo, he thought a lot of him and she had never dared to ask how much. Nowadays she did not care enough to ask. There wasn't likely to be an answer, and anyway she no longer minded. By and large she forgot about Waldo Klein. But when he was brought into her consciousness he stuck there a while.

'We'll start with melon. With ginger only,' he beckoned the waiter. 'If I have Kirsch I prefer it in a glass.'

Next morning, as he was picking up the keys of the hired car from their dressing-table he said, 'You won't change your mind and come for a drive?'

If he had said 'Won't you?' instead of 'You won't', she could have said 'Perhaps I will.' It wasn't that she wanted so much to be with him as for them to be together, as a matter of principle. She was irritated to find she had it.

And then later, after she had spread her towel on the sand and was lying face down and her shoulder-blades were prickling with the heat, she was overcome by a sense of utter deprivation. The smell of sun-oil and the parrot-cries of the beach seemed to be all she had. Or would ever get. She had had a choice and if she had made the wrong one surely it couldn't be that wrong? She opened her eyes. Beyond the border of her towel was sand. This sand did not belong to Nature. If she dipped into it she would be unlucky and come up with some piece of man-made rubbish. Broken, dirty, unmention-able things. And there was enough underneath her to people the world if people could be counted as sand, if every dry, gritty unwashed grain could count as a man or a woman.

How had she come to think that? She wasn't morbid; once she had faced facts she didn't dwell on them. Jim did, he dwelt and dwelt until a fact had ceased to be a fact or had become an entirely different one. Perhaps at this stage of their life together she was starting to take after him. Married couples did take after one another, people took after anything – some people took after their dogs.

She lifted her head. The other woman, the one she would like to be like, was standing looking down at her. She was smiling shyly. She wore a bathing-suit and her body wasn't the least bit shy. It had struck a pose, promoting itself. The thrust of the hip and the twist of the shoulders brought forward the bust: it was a nice body and worth promoting. It wasn't young and it was rather more than well-fleshed, but it was well-propped too, and without the sagging and veining Connie had to contend with. The woman was looking for something or someone. Her eyes passed over Connie without a flicker of acknowledgment. She scanned the bodies on the sand and turned towards the sea. She saw something or someone and went away down the beach. Connie watched her wade into the water up to her waist and open her arms to it with a matronly gesture. A dark head bobbed up beside her, there was a turmoil of splashing, then a pair of feet were hoisted where the head had been. The woman lowered herself into the water and swam with a strong, stately breast-stroke.

Connie stayed on the beach until the afternoon. She dozed, aware all the time of the noises around her. Why did people without their clothes sound so shrill? From time to time she turned and lay on her stomach or her back. She did not burn, she had a greasy skin which had been a problem in her youth but was now an advantage. She was roused from sleep by children scuffing sand in her face as they ran past. She sat up, chilled. The beach was half empty, people had not come back after lunch. The sun had vanished. The sky was yellow as if an egg had been cooked in it.

She went back to the hotel and took a shower. It was three o'clock. She tried on dresses to see which colour suited her best. Her suntan made her eyes look bluer, more the colour they used to be, and if her hair hadn't faded she might have passed for fortyish. But her hair had always been light, and if she were to pull out all the white hairs she had now she reckoned she would be practically bald. She frowned at her reflection. Nowadays when she looked in the mirror it was simply to check that she was decent, her dress buttoned and her face clean and a pink mouth put on. She had given up trying to make an effect; it was as if a lot which had been on the outside of her had come in. This new sudden concern with how she looked must have been picked up from the mass concern here, because people here were more concerned about how they looked than about anything else. It was catching and she rummaged through her make-up bag for an eye-pencil.

When she went downstairs to the hotel foyer it was with the firm intention of putting a name to the other woman. It suddenly became important, as if knowing what she was called would be to know what she was. The previous evening she had seen her come out of a room in the same corridor as she and Jim were in. She had noticed the number and now she went to the desk-clerk and asked, 'What is the name of the lady in room fifty-eight?'

'You wish to leave her a message?'

'No, I just want to know her name.'

The clerk consulted the register. 'This lady is with her husband.'

'And they are Mr and Mrs – What?'

'That is not the name.'

'I know it isn't!'

'If you will leave your name, madame, I will say you inquired.'

'Look, I'm staying here too, and we have met, she and I.' Connie said boldly, 'She looks like me.'

'What is your room number?'

'Forty-nine.'

'Ah,' said the clerk, 'in that room we have Mr and Mrs James Jessel.'

'*I* am Mrs Jessel. I want to know who the lady in fifty-eight is.'

'We have many hundred guests, madame. I will ring room fifty-eight and say you are here.'

'You'll do nothing of the sort!' cried Connie. 'You're being awfully stupid, I can so easily find out from someone else.' The clerk inclined his head and smiled. 'I shall report you to the manager.'

'We have a Mr and Mrs Dwight Jackson Macey from Spokane, USA –'

'Are they in room fifty-eight?'

'– but I could not say,' said the clerk.

'You couldn't say what?'

'If Mrs Macey looks like you.'

Connie felt like screaming. She also felt that she was being served right. For what had she to do with this woman? What did she hope to do? She had simply taken a notion, some sort of fancy, into her head, through really it seemed to be somewhere else, somewhere stubborn and unreasoning. From the moment she saw her crossing the hotel courtyard she had felt that this woman signified.

She went out on to the terrace and ordered tea. 'And French pastries.' Really, she thought, annoyed, what else would they be but French – in the Bai des Anges? She had missed her lunch and partly from hunger, partly from defiance, ate a mille-feuille and two strawberry tarts. Afterwards she felt calmer. Say what you like, the French couuld do some things better than anybody. But if Jim would admit that they made better cakes he would say it was a sort of thing that people could do without.

As she was finishing her tea it started to rain. The bay was blacked out by clouds which came down from the hills, changing as they came. She watched them change; they towered up in the sky and then flattened and ran out at the edges like the smoke from old steam-trains. She heard someone say, 'There's been a storm in the hills. We'll get the tail of it.'

She went back into the foyer and bought a picture postcard of Antibes in sunshine. 'Heavenly weather,' she wrote to Edith, 'I'm toffee-coloured already. The hotel is super. There's a woman here Jim says looks like me. I suppose I ought to feel flattered.' He meant her to, she could see what he was getting at. Oh perfectly! It was supposed to be a compliment, so far as it was supposed to be anything. He hadn't stopped to think, it had just occurred to him as it might occur to him that it was time to change his underwear. No, not his underwear, he had a regular system for that, a timetable. He changed his pants every other day and his vest twice a week. He simply did not know her if he really thought she looked like the woman in the green dress. And if he thought she looked like that after a lifetime together it was chilling – it was altogether freezing. 'She's not in the least like me. She's pretty and smart and about twenty years younger. Perhaps he means I ought to try more.' She looked round the foyer. The heat of the day and everybody else's warmth were being conditioned. A well-tempered breeze stirred the air just enough; they had arranged for it to be just enough for comfort. What she must do, for her own comfort, was to give him credit for a knowledge that was more than skin deep. Edith would say she must and Edith would be right. Edith had made a go of her own marriage and after her husband died had made an even bigger go of it. It was now one of the love-matches of the century.

On the far side of the foyer was the woman she knew to be Mrs Dwight Jackson Macey of Spokane, USA. Of course. It accounted for her well-fed and taken-care-of look. She wasn't pretty and smart like the woman in the green dress, the one Jim had pretended to think that she, Connie, was like, because he thought she wanted to look like that. This woman had rather muzzy features and her clothes were a convention rather than an embellishment or covering. Her body, as Connie had already seen, had nothing to hide.

Mrs Dwight Jackson Macey, at least twenty years older than the woman in the green dress, struck Connie as being twenty times more lasting. She was *whole* – a woman like that didn't leave bits of herself to be filled and ends to be tied.

She was with a young man. He was a good deal shorter than she was, but well-built in the same dependable way. His shirt was open on a brown barrel of a chest, his trousers were rolled fisherman fashion round his calves. She was holding something behind her back which he kept trying to take. She turned away from his hand each time and short of seizing and holding her in his arms he could not reach round her. His cheeks were puffed with concentration. She was laughing and bending to him with that same motherliness she had shown towards the sea. Several people were watching them, and well they might. There was something about those two which repaid watching. Without being dramatic or special, the moment was one which would stay in the memory.

The young man abruptly became still. His face darkened and swelled. He looked like a spoiled baby getting up breath to bellow. Connie smiled. But the woman stopped laughing and looked at him gravely. She touched him. It was a reassurance and an appeal. Connie could see the appeal in the way she very briefly held his chin in her fingers. He did not relax, not a muscle, so far as Connie could see. The woman turned and came across the room, straight to Connie. She stood by Connie's chair and from behind her back produced what she had been concealing. It was a picture postcard, the same view of Antibes old town which Connie had got for Edith.

Mrs Macey smiled and nodded. It was a shy smile and the nod had no certainty. 'Take it,' she said. 'Please.'

'I've already bought it.'

'You bought this one too.'

'Oh no, I didn't want two.'

'Perhaps you took two by mistake.' Mrs Macey gave the merest glance over her shoulder to see if the young man was watching. He was. She pressed the card into Connie's hand. 'We picked it up and we think it must be yours.'

'Why should it be?' Connie, looking into the woman's face, was further confused by her fixed and immutable stare. 'Well, I suppose it might be.' She added, aware that she sounded ungracious, 'Thank you.'

'You won't have paid for it, you'd better go and do that.'

'Well, of course –'

'Sometimes one forgets.' She turned to look at the young man.

Connie was puzzled. For one thing, there was no hint of an American accent, this woman sounded as English as herself. And Connie was as sure as she could be that she had taken only one card from the stand. In a curious way it was all seeming to be directed at the man, if not *by* him. Connie felt that she herself was being used.

'Well, thank you.' She picked up the postcard. 'I'll go and pay for it now. Where did you – or was it your son who found it?'

'My son?' Mrs Macey raised her heavy brows.

'The young man you were with.'

A faint but real amusement crept into the smile she turned on Connie. 'That's my husband.'

VII

When Jessel left the café the girl was on the other side of the square trying for a lift. He disliked the jaunty angle of her thumb signalling to passing cars. A truck stopped, it was carrying workmen to the building site. They tried to tempt and then to drag her aboard, but she ran laughing into the sandy alley under the trees with the boules players.

Jessel crossed the road. A black Citroën drew up. Two meaty-faced men in the front seats shouted to her and one reached an arm out of the window and opened the rear door. She hesitated long enough for Jessel to reach her side. He said, 'I thought you were going to take the bus.'

She turned to him, the laughter quenched in her face. 'There won't be any bus. It broke down.'

'It is inadvisable to accept lifts from strangers.'

'If I can get a ride to the lake I'll take it.'

'The chances are you'd never get there.'

The Citroën drove off in a blue fume. She put up her thumb again. A car swept by with a taunting blast on the horn and she gave Jessel a little push. 'You're spoiling my chances.'

A man came across the square, naked to the waist. His tight jeans cut across a crucifix of black fur which ran across his chest and down to his navel. He wore his hair in small Levantine curls. He was not young. The girl got a steady stare of appraisal; there was something derisory about the way he passed them on the balls of his feet. His buttocks synchronising, he walked to a white Maserati. He got into the car, leaving the door ajar. The girl gazed at it with an equal appraisal and Jessel was unprepared when she suddenly walked away without another glance in his direction.

He called, 'Wait – I'll take you.' She reached the car, she was looking at it, she wanted to ride in it. The engine had started and was making a soft compacted rumble like a giant purr. Jessel called, 'I'll take you wherever you want to go.'

She glanced over her shoulder. 'What are you but a stranger?'

He was hurt, which was unreasonable. When she put a hand on the door of the car he hurried to her side. 'At least you can trust me.'

'I can?' She smiled into the car at the man, then slammed the door shut, rapped dismissively on the roof and turned her back. 'OK, let's go,' she said to Jessel.

They walked out of the village. The air was like glass after the storm; Jessel felt the clarity as a pressure between the eyes, trying to break into his skull. The canvas bag hung over her shoulder. He supposed that it held the ashes. She had not used it with special deference. He remembered her throwing it before when she had climbed up to the path from the ruin, and dumping it on the floor in the café.

The Maserati caught up and inched along behind them. Jessel thought best to ignore it; the girl turned round and pulled a face. Then the driver rammed down his foot and sheared past with the engine roaring and tyres biting the road. The girl laughed. Seeing that Jessel was shaken, she took his hand. She was so small, so slight – but only in the one sense, in the other she was all consequence – she had such minimal bones and on her skin the private dew of youth. 'Why are you staring at me?'

'I was thinking I don't know your name.'

'Ruth. Where were you going – before you met me?'

'For a walk in the hills.'

'You can walk from the lake. It isn't like here, all building-lots and nature trails.'

'Shall I wait and bring you back?'

'No thanks. I'll get a lift when I'm ready.' She looked up at him, smiling. 'You mustn't worry about me. It's not your funeral, is it?'

When they came in sight of the little Renault perched on the rock she asked if it was his. 'It's a hired car, not to be compared with a Maserati.'

'Were you scared of that man?'

He said coldly, 'I merely wanted to be sure that you were aware of the risk.'

'I enjoy a gamble.'

'With your life?'

Her face changed. The tender skin darkened. 'You say that because you're old. Old people always think of death.'

Jessel was touched. He switched on the ignition. 'I think of it now and then, but no more than I have to. Getting old doesn't necessarily mean getting morbid.'

He drove the car off the slab on to the road. As she sat beside him, gripping her knapsack, knuckles white, he was reminded where she was going, and why. There was no cause for him to be touched.

They came to a fork in the road. She told him to go to the right. They skirted the base of a hill and began to climb. Gorse or ragwort, something yellow and hot, lay in quilts over the lower slopes. Jessel remembered seeing the same sort of vegetation from the window of the little train. He had looked past Mrs Klein's hat at hills the colour of mustard – hadn't everything been done by or through or because of Mrs Klein? Now that he was here again, in this country where he had seen her, not Antibes – she had been superimposed on Antibes – here among these hills he was painfully aware of her. A scent, a perfume wafting through the open windows of the car – it must, he acknowledged, come from the gorse – but old man as he was, he attributed it to her. He was still sentimental and silly enough, he was in the same sweat of fear of her. He had taken her ghost away with him like a seed and brought it back to the only place where it could germinate. Fifty years of his life annulled, he held the wheel with a boy's impressible hands.

'Why are you going so slowly?'

'I'm sorry.' He pressed down his eyelids with thumb and fore-finger and pushed them open again.

'Are you going to faint?'

'Certainly not.'

'Maurice did. We were driving down this road and he blacked out.'

'What happened?'

'I ran the car into the bushes.'

'It must have been very alarming.'

'We hit a rock and broke the exhaust. Maurice was furious.'

'What else could you have done?'

'He wouldn't believe he'd passed out.'

'I don't see how you could have avoided some damage.'

'He wasn't angry about that. He thought I could have killed him. He hoped. Not me especially, anyone would have done to do it.' Jessel was irritated to see her smiling. She had a perverse sense of humour, but perversity was the thing with young people. Their policy was primarily to upset applecarts, even Mrs Poole, agonising about her innocence. 'I had the chance and I muffed it.'

'Why should he want that?'

'I guess he was tired of waiting to die.' Jessel saw how fearful her guess had been and wondered at the difference between their ghosts. But were their fears so different? His had been of life, hers of death. Thoroughly predictable both, although he, at the age he was now, surely shouldn't be able to recall so vividly the fear he had had of living. She drew a sigh of philosophical relief. 'He managed it in the end.'

'Managed it?'

'His heart stopped.'

They began a steep run down into blue unshaven hills. Beyond, as a threat in the sky, was the razor edge of the Alps. They passed a sign warning 'Attention! Cascade', and soon entered a rocky defile. A gash of white water split the air fifty feet up. On the rocks from which it fell were daubed the words 'Oui! Mais non!' in red paint.

'This water comes from the lake. What does the priest say?'

'The priest?' said Jessel.

'Ashes to water, dust to any old place. He can't ask a blessing, it's not sacred ground. Or sacred water, is it?'

'I should imagine the procedure is short and simple.'

'I'm only going to throw them in. I can't say anything.'

'How old was Maurice?'

'Nineteen.' He judged that she must be about the same age. She held the knapsack to her. 'You married?' He nodded. 'What's her name?'

He found that he was unwilling to say. Naming Connie would be to invoke her and insist on her presence. But she had, could have, no place here. He could not get her into the context. She would be lost. He found that he was entertaining the quite extraordinary notion that Connie had a ghost which travelled and performed without the knowledge or intention of her living self, and that an appreciable sliver of it would be left to wander forlornly in these hills. It was with astonishment and solely for Connie's protection that he heard himself reply, 'Daisy.'

'On a bicycle built for two?'

He was glad to have given her cause, this time, to smile. 'She prefers the car.'

When the road began to level out she said, 'Put me down. I'll walk from here.'

'Can't I take you any nearer?'

'I want to walk.' She got out of the car, flinging her knapsack over her shoulder and he thought she was right. Human residuum was no different from any other – animal, vegetable, mineral, it was an aggregate of them all. Even one's nearest and dearest. Connie's bones, he thought with dismay, but not Mrs Klein's. 'Goodbye,' said Ruth.

'Is there anything I can do?'

'Of course not.' She turned away after a discounting glance. Jessel accepted his negligibility because she was isolated by what she was about to do. The casting of her lover's ashes set her apart, from the world, from time, from every material consideration. This was a rite of some private and beleagured faith.

Ruth. Named for some parental remorse? Or because of a need for pity – the thought, the wish that she would have pity to give? There was also the acknowledgment that she would be both instrument and victim, and a warning that by the same token, the same name, she could herself be ruthless. With a way to make she would have to be. For her it was all to do. He might guess at the rage and anguish with which she was even now preparing to do part of it.

He watched her go, the knapsack on her hip, no spreading, no wings, no joy in her bones. When she disappeared among the trees he drove on. Approaching another ridge the road snaked and merged with the limestone outcrops so that looking ahead there seemed to be no road, just rocks stacked like badly shuffled cards. The hills, drying out after the storm, presented him with a ghost that was supercharged and nearly palpable. When Waldo had ground his face into the scrub, through his pain and ignominy he had tasted the fragrance of rosemary, thyme, wild lavender and pulverised oak leaves. And been aware of Mrs Klein standing watching. Now she was conjured up in the strong ghost of the country. Her tender, ruinous essence was breathed out by this waste ground, this maquis, garigue or whatever it was called. And his skin crept as it always had when she was near. How could he account for that? He certainly wanted to account for it, he had no wish to compound the mystery of an episode which had happened fifty years ago.

He dared not take his eye off the road to look for her. The fact that he did not look was no assurance that she was not there, walking in the aisles of yellow blossom, stirring one foot behind the other as he had so often seen her. He was as afraid as he had always been, and not one iota more capable of coping with her, for all his lifetime since.

Presently he drove into the main street of St Marcuse. He recognised nothing. It was hot and pressingly quiet. Shutters were closed, a mattress hung like a tongue out of an upstairs window, chairs were tipped against the tables at a pavement café. It was not the one where he had sat drinking his coffee and wishing to be seen by Mrs Klein. The place had an air withheld and biding. Some people there were, sitting in open doorways. A man in a bloodstained apron carried a tray of pigs' heads balanced on his shoulder. The snouts nuzzled into his neck. An old woman in black crept along under a delicately trembling hat brim.

Two kilometres beyond the village was a track which he believed he remembered. It went into what was now designated 'une belle forêt, parcours pittoresque'. He drove into a clearing and stopped. The heat was moist, he seemed to be perspiring from outside in.

He got out of the car, knowing that there was no business he should have here. The trees were pines and oaks, with a grounding of thick scrub. He was soon obliged to scramble, clutching at twigs and grass to help himself up a slope. The trees leaned against the gradient. Pine-needles got into his shoes and the earth was tacky on his hands. His involvement seemed not merely unproductive but positively detrimental, even suspect.

His foot slipped, then his knees, and he lay prone, asking what he had come for. That he had come for a holiday would satisfy anyone else, even Connie. For himself it would have been a reason not to come. He lifted his face. Crouched in the scrub, his neck painfully stretched, he might have hazarded a guess. But he did not wish to guess at this moment, and could not foresee any moment when he would wish to.

He got to his feet, managing to find purchase on the slippery pine needles and polished roots. He hauled himself up the slope, hanging on to bushes which scratched and broke in his hands. More than once he lost his footing and skidded back over ground he had just climbed. It was undignified and fatiguing. His eyes misted, his heart was jumping under his collar-bone, he was obliged to open his mouth to draw breath. He did not often think of death but he thought of age, of ageing, and there had been intimations, ungentle hints of mortality. At the prospect of any major involvement he nowadays experienced an ennui which seemed to have been accumulating all his life. Yet surely it was permissible and to be expected that at sixty-five he should want to take certain things easy? In view of the fact that certain other things which hitherto had been taken easily and for granted were becoming increasingly difficult?

The trees thinned out, he came to a clearing and the sun sprang at him out of a molten sky. He had not appreciated how preferable it was to suffocate in the shade. His nose and mouth were stopped with heat, he was deafened by the insane whirring of crickets. He sank to his knees and the ground gave under him like dry toast. He rolled into the crotch of a thorn bush.

It was getting monotonous the way his nose was constantly being rubbed in the earth. The significance was crystal clear, there was no need to labour it. He scooped up a handful of earth and sorted on his palm the pine-needles and crumbled leaves, spines of broom and thorn, shards, seed-pods, grains of limestone and shreds of lichen. The answer and the question were here. He might with reason assume that his having been obliged, more than once, to put his nose into the natural detritus of these hills meant that he should accept what was under his nose. Which was simply the process of decay, the passage from entity to non-entity.

The thought had to be taken all the way. It was absolutely scrupulous and nothing, nothing within his cognisance, was exempt. He might examine in detail where that left him, but there was no necessity to do so: he could rest assured that everything was taken care of. Rest and assurance, on whatever grounds, were the most he could expect at his time of life. Also at his time of life he had no objection to annihilation.

By digging in his toes and his fingers and bending his knees he managed to get higher up the slope and came to a limestone shelf wedged into the hillside. He was able to walk along it as conveniently as if it were a pavement kerb. Presently he came to a mule-track and followed it over the ridge.

He kept his eyes lowered until he should be ready to see what lay on the other side. He never would be quite ready, but he wouldn't risk the random glance, catching but unable to sustain the sight, throwing it away because his foot had slipped or there had been some irrelevant claim on his attention. There was in fact a heap of irrelevancies. The mule-track went straight into a dump of plastic bottles, cartons, melon skins, gas cylinders, savaged copies of *Elle* and *Paris-Match*, the detritus of someone's camping-site.

After he had passed it, stepping aside to avoid soiling his shoes, the squalor communicated itself as far as his eye would reach, so he took care that it should reach no farther than his feet. Then the old stones of the track were obliterated by a raw new road and he was walking on brown earth rooted out by bulldozers. He stirred it compassionately with his foot. One might liken it to the flesh under the scabbed silver skin of the land. He was, and would always be, in a state of mortal unpreparedness. It was a disinclination, and probably prudent, to resurrect what had not been buried so much as held under.

From somewhere like this, some vantage point of memory, he stood fifty years ago looking across at the farm, at the culmination of God knew what hopes and refusals, torments and abominations. He had wanted desperately, although at that time he could not have known what he was wanting. Such things had not come within his experience, nor had they since. He would have said they were not in his nature. Yet there he had been, full of the laughter, cries, groans, whispers, creaks, crepitations, gutturals – the sounds of the celebration of love, and mingling, yet unimpeached, the essence of Mrs Klein.

He raised his head and looked for the pines. Too few to be a copse, though affording some small protection, they had been more like bottle brushes than a stand of trees. Fearing and drawn to them, as to everything connected with her, he had gone in the early morning before anyone was about and seen where she sank down, like the vapour from the little train, into the embrace of Louis or Babert or Rizzo – or unwashed old Crau, animal blood on his shirt, stains round his flies. Fifteen-year-old James Jessel had dropped to his knees and rolled himself like a dog on the ground where they had lain. And gone with the speed of a dream through processes unknown, rites of possession and defilement and the most meticulous mutilations. Then he had scrambled up and run away, running and needing to run to the ends of the earth and getting only as far as the Craus' last tethered goat because he was no good at running. Anyway, he could not escape from Waldo, Waldo's knowledge of his thoughts, which could equally have been his knowledge of Waldo's. At the time he believed that Waldo knew everything about him and he suffered for it. Mrs Klein, he supposed, had intimations of his vileness, he hoped to God that she knew none of the details. She looked at him in sorrow, but her sorrow was for the world, not just for him – he did not expect to be preferred even for his vileness – sorrow was in the arrested movements of her hands, the unwilling stirring of her feet.

La Bigorne – the house an old pink *mas* with iron brackets over cracks in the walls, and outbuildings at all stages of impermanence – had occupied the same bit of sky through sun and storm, seasons, wars, and Mrs Klein. It and its sky were gone. In their place was a complex of brick buildings with big chimneys, a car-park and an approach road through an arch studded with electric lightbulbs. Even at this distance and against this sunlight he could see that they were winking on and off, as an attraction or deterrent. He decided that he must have forgotten the exact position of the farm after all these years. But it couldn't be far away and this place was encroaching on the privacy of his memories. He continued with a sense of outrage along the bulldozed track. Drawing near to the buildings he saw signs of commercial rustic, pink geraniums and imported date palms. The car-park was full of vehicles, an excursion coach was coming along the approach road. This is ridiculous, he was thinking, I have misjudged, this is nowhere near La Bigorne.

Then he saw the pines, tenuous against the solidity of the tall chimney which had concealed them from his view.

He tried to legitimise his emotions. He could not. The new place blasphemed what had been his faith for half a century. Yet it was in the material and probably every other sense superior to the broken-down farm and the neglected terraces of the Craus. It was some sort of commercial undertaking, and successful. He had no right to despise it. As he watched, the excursion coach passed under the arch. The driver played a tune on his klaxon, the vehicle stopped and forty-three people got out. Jessel counted them. Their voices travelled, especially the women's, almost certainly American. Doors were opened to admit them to one of the buildings and he caught a whiff of intense confectionary sweetness.

Crossing what might have been this same ground, within sight of the farm, he had been aware of Mrs Klein with a sudden gruelling cognisance, not merely of her flesh, of which he was constantly aware, but of her person, her enormous prevalence. She had taken possession of all his senses. He would never be without her, he would be liable for the rest of his life, no matter how old he became. She was capable of manifesting herself at any time or place, through any sensation, and did so now through this childish smell of sweetmeats.

He walked towards the car-park. He came near enough to read the sign over the arched entrance: La Confiserie du Vieux Mas, Fabrique de confitures, fruits confits et spécialités du pays.

VIII

When Jim returned from his drive Connie scarcely gave him time to wash his hands. 'Why are you so late?'

'I had trouble with the car.'

'Trouble? For heaven's sake take it back!'

'I shall. But I doubt if there'll be a mechanic on duty tomorrow. It's a national holiday.'

'Then they must give you another car. Do hurry up, Jim, I missed my lunch and I'm dying for my dinner.'

He took up the towel. 'How did you come to miss your lunch?'

'I went to sleep.' She waited impatiently while he dried his hands, a finger at a time, as if he were smoothing on gloves.

When they sat at their table in the hotel restaurant he started to fiddle with his cuffs, poking up each wrist with the fingers of the other hand. 'What's the matter now!'

'Matter?'

'With your hands!'

He rubbed the tips of his fingers together. 'I fancy they're still a little greasy from the car.'

'What sort of trouble was it? Wouldn't it *go?*'

'Yes, but with undue noise. It developed what I once heard a Frenchman describe as "un cliquety dans le moteur".'

'If it didn't stop you or slow you down, what kept you?'

'I stopped to look under the bonnet. One never knows, it might have been something immediately visible.'

'You always fuss about the car, even when it's not yours.'

'Especially then. I was also delayed by the storm. Did you have it here?'

'Nothing to speak of. A few drops of rain, and it came over very dark. I sat in the foyer and wrote a card to Edith.' He had been gradually turning his attention elsewhere – back to his walk, she surmised – and at mention of Edith he switched off altogether and pushed a crumb about on the tablecloth. 'An extraordinary thing happened. After I'd bought the card at the desk, that woman over there – Mrs Dwight Jackson Macey I'm told her name is – came and gave me another. She insisted I'd taken two cards by mistake and dropped one.'

'Insisted?'

'I had to take the card to the desk and pay for it.'

'Well?'

'Well, it was so embarrassing! She watched to see that I paid. So did her husband.'

'Surely not.'

'I tell you I felt like a criminal!' Connie was vexed by his scepticism more than by the memory. 'I'm sure I only picked out one card.'

'You could as easily have taken two. If it was one of those display stands which swivel away when someone turns it from the other side, it swivels away before you can make your choice. You snatch at the card you think you want and take – you could take – two.'

'I didn't snatch. I was there by myself and it wasn't a stand and no one swivelled.' He raised his brows. It was a way he had of shrugging without moving his shoulders. She cried, 'They're American!'

'Dwight Jackson Macey does sound like a good American name.'

'Don't you think it was an extraordinary thing to accuse me of?'

He came reluctantly out of his abstraction. 'I'm sure they didn't mean to accuse you. It was a misunderstanding.'

'I didn't misunderstand.'

'You shouldn't let yourself be prejudiced.'

It occurred to Connie that she was covering up rather well in view of her real feeling. The reality being that Mrs Macey made her feel good. Just looking at her made Connie stop wherever she was, instead of rushing on to and relying on what was going to come next. Next week, next year. She said sharply – he was starting to push the crumb about again – 'What on earth did you do today?'

'On earth?'

'It's made you so remote. Like talking to the man in the moon.'

'I'm sorry. As a matter of fact, I had the unusual experience of being pursued by lions on the autoroute.'

'Lions!'

He told her, and Connie listened appalled. 'You must have been terrified!'

'I was worried, yes. Not knowing what the car would or would not do.'

'And you're still upset – why didn't you say?'

'I'm over it now.' He smiled his buttoned-down smile. 'The day was certainly not without incident. There was the storm, which was spectacular. And I always feel that in such violent electrical disturbances there is an element of danger. Fortunately I was able to take shelter. I had lunch while the storm was on. Afterwards I drove into the hills.'

'Where to?'

'A lake.'

'That was nice.' She thought of bullrushes and kingcups and everything upside down in the water, a lake was always nice.

'I encountered a girl.'

'What sort of girl?'

'Quite a nice sort. Very young. In her late teens.'

'Attractive?'

He shrugged with his eyes again. 'I gave her a lift.'

'Hitch-hiking is awfully risky. Good heavens, she didn't know what she was letting herself in for.'

'I think she found me tolerable.'

'Of course she was safe with you.' Connie had to laugh. Maybe she shouldn't – yet why not? Why couldn't he laugh with her? 'They're not all like you.' His eyes had become very pale, she noticed that they were quite faded. 'You must try to get a bit of a tan before we go home.'

It was young Mr Macey she looked at while they were eating. He was younger than Jim had been at any time she had known him. Or before. Jim's ears, for instance, would never have been so virginal. Did Mrs Macey call him Dwight, or Jackson? He looked like a Dwight, strong and beef-boned. 'Dwight, put out the light.' 'Dwight, don't bite!' Connie giggled. She meant it to be private, but Jim noticed. He had switched to noticing and asked what she was smiling at. 'Calling someone Dwight is a hoot.'

'Eisenhower was Dwight D.'

Connie thought that she might enjoy being married to someone younger than herself. Much younger. It could be refreshing, and sustaining. Like with these Maceys, his strength and her maturity making a good combination. He had new Yankee vigour, she had character. 'Do you think they're happy?'

'Who?'

'The Maceys.'

'Why shouldn't they be?'

'He's in his twenties and she's in her fifties.'

He hadn't noticed. He turned to look in the Maceys' direction. At that moment Dwight Jackson picked up a peach, fondled it, touched it to his mouth and put it on his wife's plate.

'I really don't see why not.'

'Of course you don't. They wouldn't make it public!' He lowered his eyes. On this stiflingly hot evening he had ordered soup and was sipping it from the side of his spoon with a judicial movement of his lips. She cried, 'Young men only marry old women for the wrong reasons!'

It was so contrary to what she thought and felt that she surprised herself. But she saw him considering it, lightly and humouringly turning it over in his mind, and when he said, 'I believe such marriages sometimes turn out rather well,' she knew that was what she was waiting for.

'They marry them for their money.' She had manoeuvred him into defending what she did not really wish to attack.

'Age is no barrier to compatability.'

'I'm not talking about just getting on together, rubbing along –' she nearly said 'like we do' – 'I'm talking about *happiness*.' He gazed into his soup. He had his own idea of happiness. She knew roughly what it was and had decided that he fairly frequently achieved it. He would common-sensibly see that he did. 'Two people enjoying life together, sharing even what they don't enjoy.'

'There's no reason why old and young should not understand each other.'

'She's not old, she's just older than he is. She must be about my age.' Connie would soon be sixty. The best that could be said for that was the knowledge that it would be ten years before she had to worry about being seventy.

He looked up with a twinkle. 'American males are said to be mother-fixated.' Connie admitted that he might have something there. She remembered how Mrs Macey had lifted the young man's chin in her hands, appealing and at the same time charmed, as by a difficult but beloved child. And the way she had opened her arms to the sea, which had probably held Mr Macey too. 'That's a rash generalisation of course. I mistrust generalisations, they are too accommodating. It is their function to accommodate.' She saw what he was doing; he was trying to deny what she might have thought he was getting at, some subtle dig at herself which she hadn't even noticed but which now she would notice, and would dig harder than he would have done. 'Whatever their reason for marrying it's not for us to speculate –'

'Let's go to Grasse tomorrow.'

He lodged his spoon across the rim of his plate. 'By all means, if we can.'

'Why shouldn't we?'

'I'd like to be reassured about the car. One never knows, it could be something which could affect our safety, faulty brakes or steering.

I shall take it back first thing in the morning. But we'll go to Grasse, even if we take the train. What a pity we can't go on the old Ligne du Sud.'

'I'd rather go by car.'

'It would not have been very convenient, in any case. We should have had to go into Nice, or Vence, to meet the train. But it was a charming little railway which ran from Nice to Draguignan and passed through some of the most beautiful scenery in Provence. I had the pleasure of travelling on it when I was here with Waldo. The line was destroyed about 1942. All one can see now are the viaducts spanning the gorges and the stations which have been turned into villas. Some of the viaducts are in ruins, some have been converted into road bridges.'

'Do you think we're happy?'

'We?'

'You and I.'

'My dear, what a question.'

'Yes, isn't it.' She waited while he found the crumb and poked it under the rim of his plate and dusted the tips of his fingers together. She guessed he was finding the whole thing distasteful.

He looked up. 'Is there some reason why we shouldn't be happy?'

Connie shook her head. She could not think of a single one. She imagined happiness as a kind of golden daze and she didn't live in that. What made it so difficult was having nothing to go by and no reason to be positively *un*happy.

He straightened his cutlery and she thought he sniffed. It would be with relief or impatience, he was not given to sighing.

'I'll have another look at the car. The system will have cooled off and it should be possible to make a closer examination.'

'I don't care if we don't go to Grasse. We can do something else. Whatever you like.' She did not say that she wanted his company. If he thought she was sorry she had let him get away on his own he would be all self-sacrificing for the rest of the holiday and refuse to enjoy himself.

'But you'd like Grasse. The very finest perfumes are made there and there are some glamorous modern shops and a flower and fruit market in the old part of the town and some nice cafés.'

The waiter brought them a dish of reddish fish with slices of lemon and what seemed to be black shells on top.

'Are those snails?'

'I think they're olives and the fish will be grilled mullet.' He sliced open one of the black things and dissected it, laying out the fragments for her to see. 'Yes, they're olives. You may take my word.'

She took it, but not enough to eat the things. She pushed them to the side of her plate.

IX

Driving back, Jessel glimpsed the girl's lake in the valley-pan. Cataracts enlivened by the storm rain leaped sheer from the hillsides. Now it must be inalienably the boy's lake. His ashes had gone into it, no one could say for sure that they were not in the mud at the bottom, or that they were. The girl had made for him a well-nigh permanent memorial. If that was what she wanted.

Now that Jessel came to think of it she had admitted that she was prepared to give the benefit of her doubt to an accredited Authority, the something more which had been organised for mankind, or which mankind had organised for itself. Superstitious or impatient, she was ready to maintain the deity in order, if he was following her confused reasoning, to provide for the old human sport of snook-cocking. It was not a laudable intention but it was prudent: better, it might be argued, to believe for the wrong reason than not to believe at all.

Taking a bend in the serpentine road he saw her running ahead, knapsack bounding like a live thing on her shoulders. He was not at all surprised. Their encounter had been inconclusive. He had been expecting to see her again, albeit with some trepidation.

Hearing the car approaching she stopped and turned. No more the jauntily cocked thumb, there was desperation in the way she flapped her hand, standing in the middle of the road. When he was near enough to see her face he was startled. Her skin was crimson and tight, her eyes stared out of cushioned flesh. She looked near to bursting.

He stopped and leaned out of the window. 'You shouldn't run in this heat,' but she was already pulling at the car door, which was locked. She actually hammered with her fists on the roof.

Jessel leaned across to put down the catch. She threw herself into the front passenger seat and crouched in a position of dire urgency not entirely due to the obstruction of the knapsack which she had not removed from her shoulders. 'Is something the matter?'

'I want to get away.'

Jessel reminded himself that it was his business only insofar as she had chosen to acquaint him of the facts: she had not invited him to share her feelings. 'You have accomplished your mission?'

'Just let's go!'

Engaging the vehicle's noisy first gear, he heard another, extraneous sound. He was immediately apprehensive but hoped it might be due to the gradient and the vibration caused by the increased revolutions of the engine.

'One little last thing and I couldn't do it. I made a complete balls-up.' She caught sight of Jessel's expression and cried, 'In case you've forgotten, Maurice is a cinder. Like the ones you put chestnuts to roast on.' Her energy packed the car, the car was full of noise and her unproductive effort. 'They wouldn't stay under water, they bobbed about like they were bread for the ducks. The ducks won't eat Maurice's cinders, they'll bob about for ever and ever. Why can't we *go*?'

'I am afraid there is something wrong with this car.'

'You know, I didn't look at them – I couldn't – they were Maurice's, I didn't think they'd look like that, did I.' It wasn't even a rhetorical question, it was a cry for help. Nevertheless he sensed a question, unformulated and unanswerable, somewhere else. Poor child, she was going to have to do so much better. One was born with this unblessed naivety and had a rough time growing out of it. 'The boatman was mad because he said they'd bring bad luck to the fishing.'

'I'm sorry.'

'I kept thinking I'm dreaming this, but it was really happening. The boatman tried to push them down with his oar. He was hanging over the side whacking the water and he burst his braces and you know what I did, I laughed. I profaned Maurice's memory.'

To whom or what did she suppose she was answerable? The shade of her lover, her conscience, or the Authority reserved for snook-cocking? Jessel put the car in motion. He hoped that when the road levelled, the metallic clattering would cease.

'It was the one other thing he wanted. People die and are buried or burned and that's it, but Maurice wanted to come here. There was always something else he had to have.' She was staring ahead, her nostrils pinched. 'Suppose they weren't his ashes?'

'Why suppose that?'

'They didn't look like ashes.'

'You have nothing to reproach yourself with.' They had been travelling downhill. The extraneous noise from the engine ceased but began again when he had to change up.

'Maurice said that what people laugh at isn't really funny.'

'Very possibly.'

'Why are you stopping?'

'I think there's something amiss.' He did not know where the bonnet-release was. Groping for it under the dash he touched her leg. 'I do beg your pardon –'

She hadn't noticed. His presence was marginal and it certainly wasn't constant. Looking at her he saw how her colour had faded, her face was grey, her lips dark as if the blood in them was bad.

'You've had nothing to eat. We'll stop at the next café and get you a sandwich.'

'What's eating got to do with it?'

'I believe it's psychosomatic.' So was his own stiffness. He moved gingerly in his seat to relieve it. His joints cracked. 'You have had a long and tiring journey and been through an emotionally exhausting experience. You need replenishment.'

'I've got masses of emotion, I'm emoted to the eyebrows.' He tried to say that food would be a mild and acceptable anaesthesia but could find no acceptable way of saying it. 'There ought to have been

[123]

someone to bless the water. I just chucked him away like we used to the ashes of our camp fire.'

Jessel wished she would talk of something else. Hers was not an emotion which could be shared. 'Years ago I stayed on a farm in this area. It was very run down, even then.' He did not know where this was leading, he felt that he himself was being pushed. 'It was not quite here, but near enough.'

'Near enough for what?'

'For ghosts.' Of course he should not have said it because she would have her own and they would be newer than his, they would still be saying what they had said in life and not what he or anyone else might impute to them fifty years after.

She uttered a sigh and seemed to shrink with it. He wondered could ashes, human or other, be expected to sink in water? If he did not know, she should, since she had often thrown the embers of their camp fire into the lake. 'You came as he asked and did your best to see that what he wanted was done.'

'It wasn't done!'

Jessel had no children and few dealings with them, but he did not miss, in her mutinously buttoned lip, her thrusting jaw and scowl, how childishly she fought despair.

'Do you think he wanted to go floating about for everyone to see? Along with all the muck? Look!' she cried as if his attention had strayed or he was disputing it, 'People throw everything in that lake. And I do mean every bloody thing. It can make you sick or it can make you laugh. Not you, though, you wouldn't laugh at love-rubbers floating in the water, would you?' She gazed at him with disfavour. 'You wouldn't be sick either, you'd stick your nose in the air.'

'Perhaps.'

'D'you think he meant he should end up like that?'

'I think you should forget the unfortunate aspects of what happened this afternoon and try to remember –' what should he recommend? The summer day, the perfumed hills – a point of effulgence which the sun had found, and only he had seen, among the unbecoming stubble of her hair? He wanted to warn her against the ghosts. Tell her that they would get old and poisonous. She could be left with secret visions, ashes floating among obscene rubbish would appear to her at inappropriate and perhaps sacred moments for ever after. History repeated itself endlessly, but not so often nor so blatantly to the eye of the informed and prepared beholder.

'I'll tell you what *I* think.' She came out of despair with the light of battle in her face. 'I think that everything – the world, the universe, the whole bang – anyway, the world – had to start right to go wrong. In the beginning, I mean, it must have been all right.' She was fighting through to something, she meant to be assured – 'Maurice has gone, he's been scrapped –' and on the way was confronting herself, as an act of courage or bravado, with a premise she could not accept – 'because he started right and went wrong. That's what everyone does. And everything. It's the only way.'

'Where does it leave you?'

'Alive,' she said sharply. 'For now.'

He had to wonder, remembering his own life-expectancy. At her age he had counted on a philosophy full of ramifications, safety-clauses and invaluable obscurity. 'I think you should remember the happiness you shared. Surely it is what he would have wished.'

She laughed, it was surprising how unpleasantly. He was surprised. On the other hand, what expectation did he have, what right to whatever was the best in her? 'Maurice said "Chuck my ashes in the water", and just then I was thinking about cooking and fires and I said "Why not just chuck the water on the ashes?" and he said "I'm talking about after I'm cremated, you silly cow. I don't want to be kept in a box. Anything left over is to go into the lake. You'd better see it's done or I'll come back and put a black on your sex life." '

X

'He was obstructive,' said Connie. 'It's not what he's paid for, it's not what we're paying for. I've a good mind to complain to the management.'

'Don't do that, it was just a mistake.'

'He definitely said you were American.'

'I don't think he could have meant me.'

'Mrs Dwight Jackson Macey – what could be more American than that? I feel such a fool. My husband did, too. He thought your husband was Dwight Jackson Macey.'

'Leslie?' She smiled lazily. 'He wouldn't mind.'

'Jim hates making mistakes. And your husband looks – well, he could be American.'

'Leslie?' she said again, with the same laziness, and it struck Connie that here was the point of all her returns.

'He looks so –' Connie thought she had better not say young – 'so well set up.'

'Clean limbed.' It was almost a drawl, but there was no mistaking the depth.

'What I mean is, apart from being misinformed, which could happen to anyone, I don't expect to be treated with suspicion if I ask the staff a simple question. After all, this is quite a pricey hotel, isn't it?' Her eyebrows went up in genuine inquiry, as if light might be thrown. She seemed to be considering a totally new concept, but with only passing interest. 'I'd better introduce myself,' said Connie. 'I'm Connie Jessel.'

'Madge Brent.' The hand she put out did not take Connie's, but followed with one fingernail the progress of a tiny coral beetle which had come out of a crack in the table. 'How pretty.'

'It probably stings,' said Connie, whereupon Mrs Madge Brent brushed the beetle to the floor and trod on it.

'I love that colour, don't you?' She lifted the toe of her shoe to reveal a small wet stain on the floor.

Connie was confused and for some reason found it a rather pleasant confusion. Perhaps she liked having her word taken. 'It was so good of your husband to see to our car.'

'He loves cars,' Mrs Brent said in the same tone as she had said that she loved the colour of coral. 'Especially when there's something wrong with them. He loves to tinker.'

'How very useful. Jim says you can't trust garages to do anything except send in their bill.'

'Leslie runs a garage.'

Connie said hastily, 'Well, I'm sure you could trust *him* – to put everything right.'

'You could, but it takes time. Time's money and people don't always want everything put right.'

'Jim does.'

'Is he willing to pay for it?'

Connie was confused again, this time less pleasantly. She looked at Mrs Brent's rings which were showy and might not be real. Mrs Brent's legs were crossed at the knee and one shoe dangled from her toe. The leather could be snakeskin – or plastic. It was hard to tell nowadays. But her safari-style dress was of real silk. For a moment Connie was ready to be disappointed, to admit that she had been properly had. It would have been justice, the way she had cherished the idea of this woman from the very first sight of her picking the head off a canna lily. 'It's a hire car, so we don't have to pay for running repairs.'

'I was speaking generally. When it comes to cars, Leslie's a perfectionist. How many people can afford perfection?'

'Doesn't he make any money with his garage?'

'Hardly.'

'That must be terribly worrying.'

'I bought him the garage for a wedding present and it's lost money ever since. Wasn't that cunning of me?'

'Cunning?'

'I reasoned he'd always want the garage but he might not always want me.' She laughed and her laughter warmed the cockles of Connie's heart. 'The more money he loses, the less hope he has of keeping the garage, unless he keeps me too. It's an insurance.' Connie knew what Jim would have said to that, he would have said that the premium was too high and he would be thinking of the principle as well as the money. A few days, a few minutes ago, she would have agreed. 'To have and to hold, unto death, that sort of keeping,' Madge Brent said and it seemed a right and quite proper arrangement. 'Every Christmas I buy him something for the garage. Last year it was a hydraulic jack for the inspection pit.'

They both laughed. Connie said, 'I think he's lucky.'

Mrs Brent opened her eyes very wide. 'Did you have to pay?' For a crazy second Connie thought she meant had she had to pay to ensure the faithfulness of Jim. 'For the postcard you took by mistake?'

'Oh yes. It will come in useful. Writing cards is a bore on holiday but people expect to get them.'

'I said to myself, someone's dropped this. Such a shame to leave it lying there to get trodden on and spoiled. It was such a nice picture of the beach.'

'Of the town, actually, the old part of Antibes. I'd already bought it to send to a friend.'

'You bought one,' said Mrs Brent kindly, 'but not that one.'

'I don't know how it happened.'

'You took two cards together, you dropped one and I picked it up. It's easily done.'

She was smiling and Connie thought how easily it all was done, and cried impulsively, 'I'm glad it happened and we got acquainted.'

'I'm always finding things. Leslie gets so cross.'

'Why?'

'You know what they say? "Lose a penny, find a pound, when love is lost it's never found." '

She gazed at Connie with thought. Connie felt that she should not inquire what she was thinking. 'Will you and your husband join us for a drink this evening?'

'We don't drink. I stopped when I was carrying my baby and Leslie stopped to keep me company.'

'You've got children?'

'I miscarried.'

'Oh, I'm so sorry.'

'It was just as well, I couldn't have coped with two.'

'Two?'

'I had Leslie.'

Connie said, 'Have tea with us tomorrow afternoon.'

'We go to bed in the afternoon.' Madge Brent, smiling, kept her eye on Connie who blinked. 'In the morning we come down around eleven.'

'Coffee then, let's meet for coffee.'

So it was arranged. Connie understood, gave herself to understand, that it was. She did not tell Jim, he disliked meeting people and these people he naturally disapproved of – even he couldn't get away from his nature.

'We'll have coffee in the garden,' she said to him the next day. 'It's the nicest place to sit.'

'It will be too hot.'

'I *adore* the canna lilies.' She caught the upward movement of his brows because it was not a word she ordinarily used. 'So does Madge Brent.'

'Who?'

'The wife of the man who was kind enough to put our car right.'

'I am not sure that there was anything wrong.'

'Knowing you, it was probably nothing to worry about.'

'Mr Brent does not know me, but he inferred that I am so ignorant about cars that it would be pointless to try to explain.'

She said reasonably, to close the subject, 'Well you didn't know what it was, did you?'

'I am as well- or ill-informed as most men who drive.'

'Cars are his business. He runs a garage.'

'It would account for his attitude. A little expertise makes for omniscience, especially with motor-mechanics. They don't credit the motorist with a grain of common sense. I have frequently had to point out that I know a plug from a piston.'

'I daresay he's conceited.' Connie did not hold it against him. Conceit was natural in a man. Jim had plenty, but shakeable. Sometimes its shakeability shook her too.

His upper lip was lengthening, the lines were etched into his skin and his mouth looked like a drawstring purse. He said, literally out of the great blue concoction of sky behind his head, 'I went to La Bigorne yesterday.'

Connie sighed. The Brents weren't coming.

XI

Jessel could see that she was taken up. He knew the signs. She was prone to sudden obliterating enthusiasms for people or policies, reversible and swiftly quenched by circumstance. She would have her reasons, which he would accept. They were unlikely to be the product of rational thought, nevertheless over the years he had found it expedient – essential, in fact – to credit her with sounder justifications than those she admitted to. Nowadays he did not ask her to admit to any.

He made no conscious decision to speak of his own reasons. He had already begun, abortively, to speak of them to Ruth. It had been a wholly physical compulsion, a spasm or eruption from somewhere unthinking – his stomach probably – and Ruth had not known what he was embarking on, nor would, nor need, have cared. Would Connie? Better judgment, any judgment at all, would have counselled him to keep quiet. But he spoke out of the same compulsion, from a need too urgent to pause and consider whether there was any prospect of its being met. He spoke sharply lest this moment, like others, should be lost. Moments were lost which he had prepared for, or seen coming, and he alone was aware of the loss. 'I think it only fair to tell you.'

'Fair?'

'Even at this distance of time.'

'You mean that place where you stayed, years ago?'

'The farm, yes.' He was checked, having to specify, but of course it was not permanently sited in her thoughts. 'In fifty years there have been far-reaching changes. The farm has gone. There is a jam factory there now.'

'A jam factory!' She laughed. 'I knew you'd go, you only came here to look for Waldo.'

What he was hoping, attempting, he now saw, was a clearing of the air, a settlement between them of his ghosts. 'I came in the hope of not finding him.'

'What's that supposed to mean?'

'I dislike him. I always have.' He was surprised at how long it had taken him to make the admission.

'Then why look for him?'

'It's not as simple as that. At my age motives get compounded.' It wasn't just age which had compounded them. There had never been anything straightforward about his attitude to Waldo. Attitude? It was more of a position. 'He was a very different person from me.' The past tense referred to Waldo and the position, for where was he without Waldo to position him? 'He was all that I am not.'

Connie said, 'Aren't you flattering yourself?'

Jessel, who had not anticipated that it would be easy, feared it would turn into a battle. 'Waldo made a success of the business of living. I saw that it could be done and that was important to me. I derived –' Not hope nor confidence nor satisfaction. 'To know him, to be aware of him, was a prospect before me. He opened up possibilities which I was able to see and to know that they existed.'

'What possibilities?'

'They were purely visionary, I could not realise them.'

'You thought the world of him, and that's too much.'

Jessel bowed his head. It was merely an acknowledgment that she had contributed to what was not intended to be a conversation. 'When I was young I was ready for anything. Later, though not eager for certain experiences, I would not have rejected them. Those which came my way I did not handle as I should wish and many I was not able to handle at all.' Connie gave him a stare of incomprehension. 'Waldo disappeared, and I found that with him things never had been as they looked to me. He left some wreckage. Really rather a mess. So I no longer have the prospect before me. Nor the solace.'

'Solace?'

'If you haven't managed very satisfactorily yourself, there's comfort in seeing someone else do so. Envy, too. I have been envious.'

'What of? What did he ever do?'

'He was good at relationships.' Jessel said wryly, 'I have always been at a disadvantage there.' He was afraid that Connie would think she ought to deny it. If she did, it would put them right back, cancel out what progress he was making. 'I'm talking about the business of living – making a life. One does try to make one. Pretty nearly the whole thing is relationships. To one another, to objects, events, places. And time. I'm finding it difficult to adjust to time.' It was what he had come here for. The situation which arose fifty years ago – half a century! – had continued, needlessly complicating and contorting itself and surely this was the moment, hopelessly belated but better than never, to resolve it. At least between Connie and himself. At most between the two of them, for who else was there? 'Waldo's mother was a very beautiful woman. She was Viennese.' At this point in time, mercifully much would be irrelevant, but he must be scrupulous in deciding what to leave out. For both their sakes he tried to rationalise Mrs Klein's beauty. 'Women of her type are often from Eastern Europe.' Warm, tender, mysterious, civilised women, the apotheosis of civilisation, one of its highest manifestations. Her charm, what he might properly call her sexuality, had seemed to him infinitely superior to the laws and practices of Nature. He still felt that to desire such a woman was the sign of a civilised man. 'They were very close, Waldo and his mother. I had no idea that such a relationship was possible. How could I, when my own parents were wholly self-sufficing? They sufficed each other, they didn't want me.'

'That's a wicked thing to say.' Connie could say it without specifying who was sinning and who was being sinned against.

'I thought it was general. You do assume, as a child, that the only way to live is the way you are living. I saw that I was superfluous and should have to make a place for myself. By the time I realised that I was more of an exception than a rule, I had formed the habit of expecting nothing.'

'And you blame your parents.'

'I don't think so. I was born with certain inadequacies and I cannot blame anyone for that. It was the luck of the genetical draw.' She looked up, almost started up, as two people approached. 'What is it?'

'I thought – never mind.'

He could have hazarded a guess but refused, at this moment. 'I learned to depend on my shortcomings. They did not fail me but I needed something positive. So I came to depend on Waldo.'

Connie was gazing after a man and woman who had just passed. The man was trying to inflate a rubber sea-horse. He had the valve in his mouth and the woman, to encourage him, was blowing into the air. Her cheeks, rounded to bursting, shone with effort. Connie's interest had been caught, which was understandable, because this was something happening before her own eyes. He was tempted to take her by the shoulders and make her listen, because he was trying to get at something which had a great deal to do with her, and with his being here. It was a recognised fact, one he had been obliged to recognise, that his serious elements were offset by irrelevancies which sometimes persisted only in his own mind. Thank God she was never to know that a vision of a wooden lavatory seat with a telephone directory hanging beside it had risen before him at his wedding ceremony, as he was about to declare 'Thereto I plight thee my troth'.

'I know what you saw in him. You put it there.'

'Perhaps. It didn't lessen my dependence, may have increased it. I knew nothing of women. I had no sisters, no female cousins or acquaintances and my mother was a closed book to me. I once met my parents face to face in the Strand and they did not acknowledge me. I don't think they recognised me, home was the only place they were used to seeing me. But had I been even as knowledgable as most boys of my age it would not have helped me to understand Mrs Klein.' Jessel summoned a smile. 'Waldo said he was going to kill her.'

'What?'

'His mother, yes.'

He had her attention although she manifestly disbelieved and had no patience with him. 'He said she was corrupt, a corrupting influence. At the time I believed that he believed it. I thought he meant to kill her and that I would be implicated.'

'How could you be?'

'There was nothing one could put past him.' Jessel reflected that now there was practically everything, he hardly knew where to begin or to stop. 'It was credible to me that he could wish to destroy his own mother. I could appreciate the reason he gave. I was too inexperienced to stop and question whether he would act from the same motives as myself. It would have been my motive, the only one I could have, in his place. In my place, the place I was then, I understood the motive but was not motivated.' He remembered her tenderness when she did not quite touch him. 'I saw no harm in her. She was a perfect woman and she brought out the worst in me.'

'What worst!'

He was amused – he ought perhaps to be vexed? – by her defensive cry. 'Perfection provokes the reverse of itself.' He had little hope that she would understand, but it had to be said in justice to them both. 'I did not want to be instrumental in her death, but I wanted what she stood for destroyed.'

'Did you?'

'It was a natural reaction. There is a balance in Nature and certainly in natures, in people's dispositions. You could say it was the correction of an imbalance.'

She cried impatiently, 'Of course you didn't kill her!' answering the question he now perceived she had asked.

'I never had any intention of doing so, nor did Waldo. It was a game, filling the time. He liked every moment filled. He told her – in my presence – that I thought he meant to murder her because of her wicked ways and they both laughed.' He remembered that her amusement had gone deeper than laughter. When Waldo stroked her nose, mocking him, there was no mockery in her smile but there was something which permanently diminished him. 'They were so very close.'

Connie picked up her bag. 'Why are you telling me this?'

'I wanted you to know how these things happen.'

'What things? Pumpkins?'

He was stopped, everything was stopped. Why had she said that? Out of what provocation – or throw in the dark? Or what insight? He did not repeat the word. To do so would have been to try to reproduce an explosion. With difficulty he got himself restarted, experiencing the same distressful battering in his chest as when he had squatted on the pumpkin in the garden at La Bigorne.

Connie said, 'I think you came here looking for her. Mrs Klein.' From her point of view it was hardly a profound conclusion, she was not to know that it plummeted straight to his monstrous childishness. Yet she had spoken as to a child, with an interest proportionate to a child's concerns, and with the customary kindness. She frowned, twisting the ring on her finger. 'Look, isn't it ridiculous, this is the only part of me that's burnt.' Her finger, pink and paunchy, belted by the ring, was like a fat, naked mannikin. He turned away, but already the image was established in his mind's eye. 'I think I know how you feel.'

'About what?'

'Getting sunburned. Look!' she said again, but gladly, 'Isn't that the Brents?'

He had wished never to see Mrs Klein again. Seeing her would almost certainly necessitate her seeing him and that, in his unexquisite shame, he could not have borne. Passing time did not weaken her influence, but served to show that it was likely to be permanent. He dreamed dreams of her which perpetuated his dismay. He did not consciously invite them, they filled him with disgust, but subconsciously it seemed that nothing was too vile for him.

After the holiday at La Bigorne Waldo did not mention his mother to Jessel or in Jessel's hearing. They spent no more holidays together. Jessel, who feared rebuff, dared not make demands and Waldo seemed disposed to let the relationship slide. Jessel tried to prepare himself to be dropped altogether, but experienced nerviness, not to say alarm, at the prospect. He could expect a profound sense of loss, indeed he had it in anticipation, without being able to decide what exactly Waldo had given him.

Their meetings after they left school were episodic and unintimate. The episodes were of Waldo's making. He was easily bored and in his presence Jessel knew himself to be boring. They went to cinemas, football and cricket matches, other people's parties and to loosely bonded clubs of unknown nature and without identifiable aims. Jessel talked when occasion permitted, about his work, his plans and anything he thought would interest Waldo. Waldo was uncommunicative about himself, from inertia, not secrecy. His affairs appeared to interest him so little that he could not bother to discuss them. He was not much taken with Jessel's, either, but Jessel himself seemed to be serving a purpose and was not yet dispensable. It was the nearest they would get to friendship. Jessel realised that in totally different ways they were both unapproachable.

One evening Waldo arrived outside Jessel's lodgings in a car. He put his finger on the klaxon and kept it there until Jessel ran out to him. The car was a black Riley with flaring mudguards and a strap round the bonnet.

'I've come to take you for a ride.'

'You can't drive.'

'I'm learning.'

'Thanks, I'd rather not risk it.'

Waldo threw open the door. 'Get in.'

'I haven't got my coat –'

'You won't need it.' Waldo pulled him into the car and even as

Jessel's coccyx, or some other vulnerable bone, hit a broken spring in the front passenger seat Waldo trod too hard on the accelerator and stalled the engine. 'Hold the choke out while I crank.'

'What?'

'Here, it's this knob. And keep the gear lever in neutral.'

'I'm not familiar with cars.'

'You'll be familiar with the coroner if you let it engage.'

The engine roared into life in a shower of sparks. 'Are you sure this vehicle's roadworthy?'

'I won a bet and the prize was the loan of one antique Riley for the evening. I thought you'd like a run in the country.'

'You mean it isn't yours? It's someone else's property?'

'Well, I'm not mad about owning things.'

The car was noisy, though it became slightly less so when Waldo had mastered the gear-changes. They drove through the City into meaner streets where their wheels slotted into tram lines.

'Where are we?'

'Shoreditch, Stratford, pointing in the right direction.'

'What for?'

'Epping Forest.'

'Tonight?' The wind was frisking the old fabric roof of the car. Waldo let the wheel spin through his hands as they rounded a corner. At the next corner only the balls of his thumbs stayed on the wheel. 'I don't think you should do that.'

'Don't you?'

'It's irresponsible.' The fact that Waldo made no comment, indirectly and by the instinct he was blessed with, served to undermine Jessel. Jessel was used to having his propositions, observations, moot points, or profoundest thoughts wither away for lack of support or attack. No matter how angry he got, and impatient with himself, Waldo robbed him of the courage of his convictions by ignoring them. He declared, 'It's childish,' and immediately felt that childishness was an enviable quality missing from his own entrenched adulthood.

'Driving a car's easy. You've got three pedals and two feet, there's not much you can do wrong, except hit an immovable object. Which you could do any time.'

'Not at fifty miles an hour.'

'The speedo reads fifty when the car's stationary.'

They plunged under a road bridge and Jessel cried out on seeing a stretch of water ahead. They hit it at speed, Jessel felt the car buck and a definite chill round his feet.

'It's only a puddle,' said Waldo.

'There's a hole in the floor – like there was in the boat.'

The memory being so much part of him he was rebuffed when Waldo said 'What boat?'

'The old tub we went out in when we were staying at La Bigorne. Don't you remember?'

Waldo said as if replying, 'She never married.' Jessel's heart turned over with shock. Yet he had been waiting for this since he last saw her sitting smiling her meshing smile. 'She should have, don't you think? A woman like her.'

'Like what?'

'You know as well as I do she's a whore.'

Jessel was not by nature violent. There had been occasions when he had wanted to hit Waldo. Visualising the blow had always sufficed. He saw it as glancing, slipping off, missing its aim, losing its impetus because the adrenalin would drop in his arteries at the very moment and by the very action of putting his fist up.

He wished that he could be rash and imprudent and hot enough tempered to strike now and damn the consequences. If he struck now, Waldo would not be able to laugh it off – moving at speed Jessel would be a dangerous man.

'Got any money on you?'

'A few bob.'

'We'll have to buy petrol. A couple of gallons should be enough to get us there and back.'

'Where's there?'

'Ongar. That's where she's living.'

Something, his gorge probably, leapt into Jessel's throat. 'She?' He would at least make Waldo identify her – if only as his possession.

'It's not a retreat, she isn't finished.'

'Who are we talking about?'

'She took a fancy to you. "My unlaughing cavalier" she called you. "What he lacks in humour he'll make up for in passion." She really believed it. She wants to see you again.'

'I don't want to see her.'

Waldo let the wheel slip through his fingers. 'Ungracious bastard.'

'It's nothing personal –' Jessel, trying to approximate to the truth, was conscious of a dampness reaching down to his bones – 'not to her. Personal to me.'

'She's right then, you're a hot little number. They say lizards can smell water in the desert.'

'I'd be obliged if you'd stop the car.'

'We're almost out of gas.'

'What's that got to do with it?'

'Restarting uses more petrol.'

'Then turn around and go back.'

'Why?'

'Because I don't want to go on.'

'If we don't find a garage we won't be going anywhere.'

Jessel hugged his knees, keeping his feet clear of the floor. The needle sank on the gauge and then jumped back to the credit side.

'I know you're uncontaminated,' said Waldo, 'but it's up to me to object. Which I have done and would still be doing if I thought it would do any good. But here I am, twenty-two years old, which makes her forty-five, and if anything it's worse.'

'Worse?'

'Because I understand now, I can see her problem. It's no different from mine, except in degree. And sometimes,' he turned

[140]

on Jessel a calm, sombre stare, 'I'm not sure which of us would score the most. Except she's been at it longer.'

'At what?' Jessel was bitter, knowing from experience that serenity was a minefield and might at any moment explode in his face.

'If she'd been a man she'd have a good name. People respect men for it, they laugh but they think it's commendable. I know how she feels, which is more than you do, but I'll see her damned for it. Bloody unfair, isn't it?'

'It's nothing to do with me.'

'Ah, here's a garage.' Waldo turned in beside the petrol pumps.

'Are you going back or aren't you?' Waldo shrugged. 'Promise, swear to me you'll turn round and go back!'

'Oh I'll be going back. *I'm* not staying the night.'

He was amusing himself, and the civilised world. The uncivilised would probably appreciate it too. Jessel got out of the car and ran.

XII

Leslie Brent wore swimming trunks, his wife her blue sundress, a straw hat slung by a ribbon across her throat and hanging between her shoulder blades. Connie called to them or they would have drifted on to the beach.

'We waited coffee for you.'

'We had coffee,' said Leslie Brent.

'You were to have it with us – I thought.' Connie looked at Madge Brent.

'Car OK?' said Leslie to Jim who had risen from his chair.

'I haven't tried it on the road. Do sit down, Mrs Brent. I'll order coffee.'

When he was out of earshot Connie said, 'He thought there was something wrong and that's as bad as if there was. He worries.'

'That little motor will take you anywhere, so long as you don't get a puncture, blow a gasket or skid on a chip butty.' Leslie turned one of the chairs and sat astride it, facing Connie.

'You've set his mind at rest.' Connie's wasn't. Leslie Brent was what they call all male, right down to the black hairs sprouting from his toes.

Jim came back saying, 'The coffee won't be a moment.'

There was an awkward pause. Connie found it awkward but she could see by the way Jim pinched up the knees of his trousers and laced his fingers that he found it gratifying. Leslie Brent folded his arms on the back of his chair, lowered his head and whistled into the hollow of his elbow.

'Have you been to Grasse?' said Connie. 'We're going this afternoon.'

'A fair old stink,' said Leslie.

'I've never been one for scent.'

'Be careful what you buy,' said Madge. 'Some perfumes aren't the same when you get them home. Especially if you live in the north. They can't rise to themselves in the cold and damp.'

'Nothing I buy is the same when I get it home. Dresses and hats, shoes. Even Hoovers.' Connie caught Jim's look of disbelief. Yet it was true and he always said, in a voice of reason, 'Why did you buy it if you didn't like it?' and she always said, 'I liked it when I bought it.' What he could not believe was that she could bring it out now, discrediting them both – he would think she was – before total strangers.

The coffee came and while she was pouring it she asked did they live in the north.

'Spennymoor,' said Leslie. 'In the real country.' He lifted his arms and legs, balanced on his buttocks and frankly stretched himself. 'Cold and wet and smelly.' Connie met his passing look, it was too passing to read but it flustered her. He snatched back a yawn. 'I'll go for a swim.'

'Mrs Jessel has ordered coffee for us.'

'Too much coffee goes through me like a dose of salts.'

'It doesn't matter!' cried Connie. 'About the coffee, I mean –'

He blew out his cheeks and scowled with the thunderous look that babies have before they roar. But between his brows was a knot which was far from childish.

'Darling,' his wife said softly.

It was a call and he answered it. His face cleared, he smiled at Connie and raised his cup. 'Made from the best Cascara beans.'

Connie felt Jim's disapproval. Her right side was cold with it, she just hoped that Madge Brent, sitting on the other side, didn't feel it too. Leslie Brent was no company for Jim, but who was?

'Jim came here when he was a boy and this is the first time he's been back.'

'You must notice some changes,' said Madge Brent.

'I spent but a few hours in Antibes and scarcely remember it.'

Connie said, 'What *do* you remember?' His smile was so thin that she could see his bones in it. She was unable to stop herself, 'The Kleins!'

'Who?' said Madge.

'He stayed on a farm with someone called Waldo Klein and his mother. I never met her, but Waldo and his wife Daisy are rather a funny pair.'

'Funny?'

'Well, eccentric.' She could see that Madge Brent wasn't interested and Jim was coldly angry. Something had got into her and was telling her what not to say. She had these little spats occasionally. But not when other people were present. The Brents had set her off. The more she avoided looking at Leslie Brent's knees and Madge's smile which was like the Mona Lisa's, signifying whatever she, Connie, might like or would rather it didn't signify, the more she had to keep on about the Kleins. 'Jim, do you remember that bead curtain in their hall?'

'Bead?' said Madge.

All that Connie had against them was that their name was sacred to Jim. They were the only people he had time for: years, donkey's years he had had for the Kleins. 'It was straight out of the Twenties. And they're not that old. It wasn't their period, so they couldn't have got stuck in it. I said to her once –' it was only the once that she had met Daisy Klein – ' "You don't see many of these bead curtains now", and she said, "We like it, it reminds us of an opium den." '

'If such a remark was made,' Jim said, 'it was meant as a joke.'

'Oh it was made, but she wasn't joking. I never heard her make one single joke. That was *his* department.'

Leslie, who was rocking his chair backwards and forwards, said, 'A laugh a minute,' to nobody in particular.

Connie saw Jim's jaws tighten. 'I wonder what's happened to my ring!' She looked under her saucer.

Leslie said, 'Ring?' Madge said, 'Happened?'

'I took it off, my finger's sunburned and quite sore. It's on the table somewhere.' She pushed aside the crockery and shook out the paper napkins.

Leslie stopped rocking. 'What ring?'

Connie knew very well where it was. She had dropped it into her bag when the Brents arrived. This was a ploy to stop Jim from bringing out one of his acid comments. She wasn't sure how much Leslie Brent would take.

'It's a hoop of small pearls, old and worn very thin and cuts into my finger. I shouldn't keep wearing it, but it belonged to my mother.'

'You mustn't lose it,' said Madge.

'I can't have lost it.'

'What do you mean by that?' said Leslie.

'I mean it's around somewhere, it'll turn up.'

'Where will it turn up?' He was staring at her and he wasn't the thunder-baby, the knot between his eyes had grown so big as to be almost a deformity.

'It can't have gone far. It was here five minutes ago. Perhaps it rolled away, rings do. It's so ridiculous, isn't it, to get a sunburned *finger*. Really it's quite painful –'

'Why don't you look for it?' Leslie Brent said to his wife. 'Why don't we all look.' He began shoving the coffee things about so that the cups rocked in the saucers and the coffee was spilled and dripped off the table. 'Why don't we turn out our pockets?' He forgot he was wearing only swimming-trunks and plunged his hands at his thighs.

'It might be a good idea to look in your handbag,' Jim said to Connie.

'Oh I'm not worried. It'll turn up –'

'Like hell it will.'

'May one ask what you mean by that?' Jim said coldly.

'It better had turn up is what I mean.' Leslie Brent kicked the chair from under himself with a throw of the leg and stood up. Without another look he went down the path to the beach.

'Oh dear,' said Connie.

Jim picked up her handbag from under her chair. 'Will you look or shall I?'

'I will.' She snapped open the bag and felt inside. The ring had fallen among the papers at the bottom of the bag. 'There!' She opened the pages of her passport and showed them the ring. 'I knew it would turn up.'

Madge Brent said, 'That's a nice picture of you.'

Jim said, 'I think you had better give me the ring for safe keeping until you are able to wear it.' Connie meekly handed it to him and they watched him stow it away in a compartment of his wallet. 'Now, if you will excuse me, I shall go to the desk to inquire if the newspapers have arrived. There was some sort of local hold-up in the delivery this morning.'

He went, with his walk like scissors, which was more pronounced when he was annoyed or embarrassed. Connie could hear the rasp of his trousers fabric as one leg sheared past the other. 'I've upset him. Your husband too.'

'You didn't upset Leslie, I did.'

'You?'

Madge rummaged in her own bag, took out a cigarette and lit up. 'He upsets me. We upset each other. That's only natural.'

Connie, who had always thought that Nature was quite enough, sighed. 'Jim never quarrels. And I can't on my own.'

'We don't quarrel, we fight.'

'What's the difference?

Madge Brent smiled. 'Surely you know.' Connie, finding that she did know, felt hot, starting from a place which she would not have wished to specify. 'Men and women have certain biological requirements, fighting satisfies some of them. I'm twenty years older than he is. As you must have noticed.'

'I haven't given it a thought.'

'If you haven't, it's no credit to me. A twenty-year-old – any twenty-year-old – has time on her side. Time's the best ally, better than looks. She doesn't have to lift a finger.'

[146]

'Not a finger, no,' said Connie, surprising herself. They both smiled. 'Jim was annoyed with me. He hates bothers.'

'Leslie will sulk for a while. Scowl and kick his feet. When I first saw him do that I thought he was fooling and I laughed. He nearly killed me.'

'He *was* angry about the ring.'

'Your ring? No. It was something else. It started this morning in bed.' She exhaled smoke with a tranquil sigh. 'It will probably finish there.'

Connie looked to where the sea showed as a blue bodice between the walls of the redoubt. She thought that Jim must have corrupted her in some subtle and proper way. Because she was strongly and not at all decently affected by thought of the arrangement made for the human race by forces out of that race's control.

He personally found it undignified and would not share his indignity with her. He was as thoughtful and humble with her afterwards as if they had just been passionate lovers. Though how, thought Connie, was she to know about passion? And at this time of life she wasn't likely to get to know. It was her turn to sigh, but she didn't. She looked at the blue bodice of sea and hoped that perhaps it came to the same thing in the end. During the first days of her marriage, hadn't she been quite happy to be happy, thinking that was all there was to it? If she had never been told there should be more, wouldn't she have settled for what she was getting?

'Let's go and see what Leslie's doing.'

'I'd better not come.'

'It will look better if you do.'

'Why?'

Madge dropped her cigarette into her coffee-cup. 'If I go alone it will look as if I can't do without him for five minutes.' She held out her hand. 'I'd sooner he didn't know that.'

They went to the beach. As they picked their way between the sunbrellas and the bodies, Madge said, 'En masse I think temptation loses its grip, don't you?'

She went to the water's edge with the leisurely motion of her hips which soft sand underfoot could not balk. They found Leslie Brent crouched, chin on knees, staring out to sea. His back was holed with broken blisters, and bright pink. Madge stood beside him and gently spread her finger-tips between his shoulder-blades. It was a healing gesture. He did not look up.

'You're going to be terribly sore.' She said to Connie, 'He only uses oil for his engines.'

'My ring turned up,' said Connie. 'I knew it would.'

He said something which she didn't hear. Madge went down on her knees beside him. 'It was in her handbag.'

'I'd slipped it in when you came. Not thinking,' said Connie, 'or rather I *was* thinking, I suppose.'

He turned and looked up at her. 'Thinking what?'

'That it might get lost or dropped and trodden on. It could easily be overlooked.'

'Everything's all right,' said Madge. 'Everything's fine. I promise.'

'You and promises!'

'I'm keeping this one.' She stroked his mouth, softening it. Then she opened her lips and closed her eyes and kissed him. It was a long kiss, but no one on that beach took notice. Connie watched blankly, feeling herself getting blanker, as if she had been switched off and could not register anything except the sand burning her feet. She thought desperately of her feet.

Madge and Leslie Brent drew apart. He stood up in a single movement and walked into the sea. He swam out and began turning somersaults. They watched his splashes glittering in the sun. Connie lifted her feet one at a time for relief from the hot sand.

Madge said, 'Seawater's good for sunburn. It's the salt. Didn't they use to rub salt on wounds?'

XIII

'It's not going to start again, is it?' Leslie Brent said, seeing her feeling in her purse, touching the flower head and putting it aside for the five-franc piece for the magazine she wanted to buy.

'What?'

'You know damn well what.'

'No. Tell me.'

She could be calm and casual as you like, but not to his liking. He took the purse out of her hand, turned it upside down and let the contents – coins, keys, everything – fall to the floor. People looked round to see what the clatter was. He kicked at the flower head.

She said, 'My dear, we've been over all that.'

'Let's go over it again.'

'It was out there in the courtyard, beside one of those tubs. It had dropped off the plant. Or someone had knocked it off –' she started a smile – 'I don't mean stolen. Who would want to do that? Someone had broken it off, one of the children perhaps, it's such a pretty colour. I couldn't leave it to die.'

'You picked it.'

She sank on her heels, smiling at him as she went down, with a submissive, charming movement that was almost a curtsey. It turned his loins to water. She picked up the flower first, then began to gather up her money. The reception clerk came from behind his desk to help her.

Leslie Brent went into the dining-room. Two young boys were stripping the paper covers off the tables. They screwed up the covers and shied them at each other, hardly bothering to take aim. It was a declaration of independence. If he had been in charge he would have smacked their bottoms.

He perched on one of the tables so that when they got to it they would have to ask him to move. As they worked nearer they laughed. The bigger of the two balled-up a table cover and threw it into the air so that it fell in Leslie's lap. Leslie seized it, wadded it hard and aimed. The boy took it squarely on the nose. His retaliation was swift and joyful. The other lad joined in and the three of them pelted each other. Leslie's teeth were on edge. He used the full force of his arms and the boys yelped like puppy-dogs. Finding himself short of a missile he picked up a wooden pepper-mill.

He scored a hit with it. The smaller boy got it in the chest. He grizzled and cringed with his hands over his eyes. Leslie was suddenly sick of himself and of the whole business. It had become a business which he had to work at, and throwing paper balls was an attempt to work it off. Without success.

'OK, kids, that's it.' But when he turned his back he was hit in the neck. He whirled round. 'Finito!' and put up his fist. It wasn't these poor little shags he should punish, it was her. She was in the doorway, watching. 'Toot finito. Compri?' He went to her, stood nose to nose. 'I ought to beat it out of you.' She blinked, but not distressfully, and took his fist and opened it a finger at a time as if they were playing a finger-game.

Behind them the boys were giggling. He looked round as the bigger one held out his hand to the other boy who rolled his eyes and kissed it.

Pushing her before him he steered her across the foyer towards the garden. His arm was locked in hers and she was gazing up at him, they must look a devoted couple, nobody would guess what he was working at. He took her to the end of the paved walk and held her with her back against the balustrade that ran around one side of the garden. 'I saw you pick that flower.'

She put her head back. He was directly in front of her. He knew about the line of her throat. The first time he saw her, her face was upturned to watch a flight of birds and her throat had seemed to yearn towards it. He could see it now, soft and full and more naked than the whole of the rest of her. 'Listen –' he shook her because she needn't be listening, 'you picked it, you took it.' She had shut her eyes, counting on getting him to kiss her: kiss and make up she was thinking, that's the way with him. 'You bitch, you promised!'

'You're hurting me.'

'You picked that flower, you stole it.'

'The flowers are for everyone.'

'You stole from everyone. You took it from where everyone could see it and hid it. For yourself.' It was a small simple fact which boiled down into the one big, ugly mess.

'Oh Leslie.' She could smile and sigh his name and make him feel like her own private fool. He pinned her against the stone, the edge caught her in the small of her back and she winced. 'If you'd picked it and thrown it away I wouldn't give a sod, but keeping it, putting it in your purse with your money makes you a common thief.'

Her eyes were pressed shut, tears pricking through her lashes. 'Why would I want to steal a flower?'

'Are you asking me?' He dropped his hands and moved away, remembering, if it wasn't too late, that he couldn't rely on himself while he was touching her, even in anger. She could get to him through a smack in the face.

She opened her eyes without rebuke and straightened her shoulders, then her dress. 'I must pass those flowers dozens of times a day, I often look at them and sometimes I touch them. But I've never picked one.' She put a hand to her hair, resisting – he guessed she was – the need to touch the place on her back which he guessed was painful and, would he believe it – oh yes, he would! – he wanted to do it for her, to ease the hurt.

'Yesterday it was the postcard.'

'That wasn't me, you saw who that was, you saw her go and pay for it.'

'It's all going to start again. I know.'

'Oh my dear.' She put into the words everything she felt and made him feel, love and sadness and enough hope and fun to be shared between them. She was handling him, it was what he had married her for.

The Renault with its bonnet up in the hotel car-park drew him like a magnet. Someone had his head inside and was feeling among the distributor leads as if he was looking for a soft centre in a box of chocolates.

'Trouble?' The man straightened up, he was old and pale as junket. Leslie had seen him in the hotel. 'Won't she start?'

'The car starts quite well, thank you.'

'So what's bugging you?'

'I beg your pardon?'

'Transmission, fuel, clutch?'

'I have yet to discover.'

Leslie looked at the engine. The wiring was a spaghetti riot, the cables were bright yellow and someone had sloshed phosphur paint into the wheel arches. 'They've had fun, haven't they? Did she pack up on you?'

'No. But there is a noise which I find rather worrying.' Leslie leaned into the engine and pulled off one of the plug leads. 'I can't say whether it's normal in a car of this kind. I have hired it and I only took delivery today.'

Leslie wiped the lead with his thumb. 'Start her up and let's listen.'

'It's very kind, but I mustn't detain you.'

'I'm not going anywhere. Try with the clutch out and no choke.' He snapped the lead back on the plug. When the engine fired it sounded happy enough.

'I have no fault to find with the performance. The noise is audible only when the car is in motion.'

'Are there any tools?'

'An emergency pack. But please don't trouble yourself. I'll take the car back to the agent in the morning.' Leslie picked out an adjustable spanner and adjusted it. The old fellow rabbited on. 'I am not questioning your expertise, but in the case of a rented vehicle one has certain rights and certain limitations. The hirers undertake to rectify faults which develop in normal use, it is what one pays for. I do not think we should attempt repairs, even with your good offices. It could provide a loophole for evading responsibility.' The spanner slipped and Leslie cursed. 'Please be careful, you may do some damage – to yourself no less than the car. The agents indemnify themselves against unauthorised work –'

'I think you'll find you've lost your rattle.'

'Oh. What was it?'

'Nothing special.' The speciality was that the plugs were hairy, the fan-belt worn, the engine-block bleeding oil. But those needn't be immediate problems. The car could soldier on for a few hundred miles and the old fellow was nervous already. He reminded Leslie of a teacher at his school who was forever slapping his own wrists. 'Could have been the air filter.'

'The air filter?'

'Or the battery loose in the housing. Take her round the Cap and see if you hear anything.'

'I think not. I have had enough driving for today.'

'Like me to try?'

'Thank you, no.'

'It's OK, I wouldn't scarper with it. I'm staying at the hotel.'

'Of course I didn't mean – I wasn't implying –' He would have reddened if he'd been the reddening sort. He clasped his hands, it really bugged him to feel the grease on his fingers. 'I do beg your pardon. Mr Macey, isn't it?'

'What?'

'You are Mr Jackson Macey?'

'No.'

'Then – I beg your pardon.'

'My name's Brent.'

'But I understood – I was given to understand – that you are from the United States.'

'Never been there.'

'I'm so sorry. My wife, I thought, had it from your wife.' He made his disapproval plain. 'My wife dropped a picture postcard and your wife picked it up.'

'And?'

'Your wife said you were Mr and Mrs Jackson Macey from Spokane in the United States of America.'

'Our name's Brent and we're from the UK.'

'Obviously my wife was under a misapprehension.'

'Or mine was.' Leslie pulled the tail of his shirt out of his trousers and wiped his hands on it.

'The onus is on our side,' said the old man, stiffening like a beetle.

'Onus? You think we haven't got one of those?'

'It was simply a mistake, Mr Brent –'

'She'll have an answer, she always does.' It had better be one he could accept. When she pulled his leg she couldn't see that she was pulling his whole anatomy.

The boats in the harbour rode a wind that had come in overnight and was pinching the water up in peaks. Leslie, who had once worked on a North Sea fishing boat, thought of storms in the Skaggerat. He had been unprepared for violence in Nature. His own he knew about and had seen others', but people had reasons for what they did. The unprovoked assaults of water, wind and sky which didn't even combine, just fought for the privilege of breaking his ship, and meanwhile, until the whole lot was sent to the bottom, smashed crockery, spilled food, knocked his feet from under him and generally stood creation on its head, hadn't scared him. He had been thoroughly indignant.

Boats in this Mediterranean harbour had bells on their masts, tinkling bells like the ones round the necks of poodles, which was what they were, poodle-pets of rich men.

'What are you smiling at?' said Madge.

'Did I ever tell you I once saw a mate of mine drown in a cup of tea?' She didn't know where to go from there, and looked at him, wondering. 'We were at sea in a storm. Everything had gone mad, including the gauges. This fellow, a leading stoker, was going round dead on his feet. So were we all. He was given a mug of tea, he took a swallow, the boat stood on end and the tea went the wrong way. It got into his lungs and he couldn't breathe. Not an easy death, drowning.'

'Leslie, what's the matter?'

'Nothing that I know of. Do you know of anything?' He had done all the talking he wanted to do and it had got him nowhere. He would have bet, though, that the talk had left her well placed in her own estimation. 'Let's walk round and look at the toys.'

'What can I do?' She did not tan or redden. Her skin was the same dense, warm, creamy colour as it was at home, except under her eyes where it was slightly pouched and blueish like thin milk.

'You've done enough.'

'What can I do to make you believe me?'

'You'd like me to believe you, wouldn't you?' So would he. At first he had never dreamed of doubting her, he had been like the ostrich swallowing alarm clocks. And the alarms had gone off, one after the other, inside him. 'Are you coming?'

'I'm rather tired.'

'Go and sit in the café over there.' He turned and walked away.

'To make you believe me,' she said, as if he wasn't trying, as if he had to be forced. Look at this morning, the business with the ring. When she came to him on the beach he had believed her. It was the way she and the other woman looked at each other, thick as thieves, that gave him to think again. He thought how she could have said to the woman, I picked up your ring without thinking, I'm always picking things up, I don't notice I've done it and my husband gets so angry. So please don't tell him. And the woman, wife, as it turned out, of the old stick with the car, would have believed her. Anyone

[155]

seeing her loaded with rings like she was wouldn't dream she would want to knock off another. 'I wish you wouldn't use that expression,' she said to him once. 'OK, I'll stay "steal",' he said, 'because you do, you bloody steal.' She had laughed. 'Darling, how you exaggerate. Why on earth should I steal? I can afford to buy what I want.' And then he had said, it had been on his mind and he had to say it, 'Women do when they get to a certain age. I've read in the papers about rich women stealing tins of beans and packets of soap powder.' 'Oh Leslie, Leslie –' the tears of laughter stood in her eyes, 'those are unhappy women, sick women who are missing something in their lives. I'm well and happy, I have everything I want.' She had added, certifying it, 'I have you,' and he had shouted at her, 'Not much longer if this goes on!' She was putting them both at risk because she was the only one who could handle him. It had been, and still was, high time somebody did. His own mother hadn't been able to, even when he was a babe in arms. Madge was the one; in or out of her arms, Madge could handle him.

But this place had taken him out of himself and, worse, out of her. It showed how easily it could be done, which was the very last thing he needed reminding of. This place was a complete phoney, they ought to have gone to Blackpool where the nonsense was straight nonsense and kept separate.

Thinking of the old dogger he had sailed in, built like a fortress, iron-timbered and stinking, he spat in homage to her memory. These toys might venture out on fine days, swell ritzy sails and flash their chrome about and if there wasn't breeze enough, switch on their motors and make frilly water round the Cap.

There was a party in progress on one of them, men and girls dancing on each others' necks to a singer with a voice like a chainsaw. Not the kind of thing he fancied. A girl waved to him. He waved back though he didn't fancy her either.

There must have been hundreds of boats, two- and three-masters, schooner types, sloops, yachts and cabin cruisers with striped deck awnings and pennants and brass riding lamps. Boats

from South Africa, Ireland, London, New York, Cowes, Gothen-
burg. He walked round, looking about, asking himself what did he
know. He thought he had seen enough to be going on with in this
fraud of a place and he had not been in two minds about what made it
tick: money to spend. What he was seeing now, in the sort of
artfulness he could put a price on, was how money could be thrown
away.

One boat stood out from the others, a small ketch, blazing white,
no flags, bells or canopies on her, just the main and mizzen masts
and their ropes. The deck was pale ash colour, the deckhouse and
rails varnished wood, the bollards stainless steel. On the hull was the
name 'Batavia'.

It's nice, thought Leslie, approving everything about it. He would
have liked to see that strong hull in the North Sea, knifing the grey
swells.

A man came on deck. Leslie called up, 'Nice boat.' The man
nodded. Leslie walked to one of the power and water meters on the
dock and sat down to take a longer look. He didn't covet the boat, he
never coveted other people's possessions. He reasoned that he had
enough and saw to it, or tried to, that what he had gave him all he
wanted. Madge called it making do. 'There's no need' she said, she
couldn't see that he got satisfaction from it.

He looked for the most in everything and sometimes it was given
him with no sweat. Like the sight of this boat. He wished Madge was
here to share it with him, he would have to tell her about it but he was
not good at description. What tonnage would it be? He got up and
went to the edge of the dock to see how she lay.

The water was bottle-green but the boat's draught was shallow
enough for him to see down to her keel, larking gently in the light
from above. How could he tell Madge about that?

The man on deck said, 'Come aboard if you like,' and Leslie
didn't need asking twice.

It was more years than he cared to remember since he last felt a
boat deck under him. At that time it had put him on his mettle to

think that there were only a few planks between him and room – about three-quarters of all the room in the world – to die in. Not that he was nervous, he was just acknowledging the fact that until he stepped ashore again he was going to be on sufferance, and a hell of a lot of that he could expect from the sea.

Now he got a touch of the old feeling – about as much as an airman might feel on a fairground swing. It was no reflection on the Batavia. Nor thanks to her. It was due to the fact that the companionway was down and one foot, so to speak, was still on the shore.

She didn't smell like any boat he had been on. The old dogger had had a stink a mile high which the North Sea couldn't sweeten. Here, he smelled varnish, and coffee was brewing in the galley.

'Nice boat,' he said again. The fellow who had asked him aboard was leaning on the rail, looking over the dock. 'Mind if I look around?'

'Feel free.'

Leslie admired the way the boat was maintained, even though it didn't work for a living and had probably passed the winter in dock under dry covers. The deck was clean enough to eat your dinner off it and the only greasy mark would be from the gravy. The layout was practical – pleasure would have to be practical for the sort of people who ran these boats. There was a shelter cabin-cockpit separated from the main housing by the motor-cockpit. The steering, being just abaft of midships, would give less motion in a seaway and maximum visibility under power or sail. The standing rigging and halyards were of stainless steel. The sails themselves were stowed on the forward deck with the chain and anchor locker next and a small cage on the forepeak where the girls could stand to catch the spray. There was a collapsed rubber dinghy in a bin on the prow with its out-board motor beside it. The pale blue anti-knock bags were at salient points, not cluttered all over the hull as they were on some of the boats.

'What's her power? Twelve horse, two-cylinder?'

The man turned himself round. He put his elbows on the rail and leaned his back against it, facing Leslie. He was young, slimly built, lazy boned. He asked, 'Have you a boat?'

Leslie was going to reply politely when he saw that the fellow was batting his eyelashes at him. 'Only a sauce-boat. Mind if I look at the engine?'

'If you want to.'

'I'm generally interested in anything mechanical.' Leslie went over to the engine pit. He lifted the hatch. 'My, look at that! That's a honey. Beautiful.' He meant the beauty of organisation. For him, looking at an engine was looking at the realisation of a dream – hadn't it been the dream to get heavy objects moving, not of their own accord, but of man's? He loved the compactness, and the co-ordination of an engine was better than Nature's, the hip-bone connecting to the knee-bone and the knee-bone connecting to the ankle-bone was nothing to the way a carburettor worked.

'What's your name?' said the young man.

'Brent.'

'It suits you.'

Leslie stooped into the engine. 'I'll bet this is a Lowry-Salmson. No one else makes them like this. That check pipe – it's original, I've got to say.'

'Brent what?'

'Just Brent.' He felt a touch on his backside, he could have sworn it was a touch. He swung round. The young man smiled.

'Where are you from, Just Brent?'

'North. Where are you?

'The home counties.'

Somewhere in Shitshire, thought Leslie. He turned back to the engine. 'What's her top speed?'

'I've no idea.'

'Six knots, five and a half –'

'I own the boat, other people sail it.'

'It's all taken care of.' Leslie was getting his fingers in. 'A flexible

[159]

fuel pipe next to the engine because of vibration – is the shut-off valve vacuum or electric?'

'How should I know?'

'You should know what you pay for – apart from anything else.'

'Ah, but I do know about anything else.'

'It's the packless type. What about reduction gears?'

'What about them?'

Leslie straightened up. 'Don't you even know if you've got them?'

'Naturally I've got them. And graduated cocks with fully-fledged T-bolts and self-adjusting plimsolls.'

'What?'

'Haven't you heard of the plimsoll line?'

'That's a load-line –'

'Quite: the plimsolls adjust to the load so that if everyone suddenly goes up front the boat doesn't stand on its head.'

He looked at Leslie through his lashes. Leslie longed to slap him on the nose. He dropped the grating hatch back in place. 'Thanks for letting me look.'

As he went down the companion-way the man called after him, 'We're going to Genoa, you can come if you like.'

Walking off the dock Leslie saw the guts of some large animal, a cow or a horse, swollen white in the water, one of the pipes poking out like the periscope of a submarine. He thought how he had talked about fuel lines and shut-off valves and could have kicked himself.

When he told Madge about the Batavia he didn't mention the owner's fairy-ness. She listened, her eyes on his face. She had a way, when he talked, of opening visibly. It was not an easing-up so much as an easing-on and he didn't think she knew she was doing it. It was an invitation, it was her body signalling. Her mind, he had to believe, was on what he was saying. He knew why she did it and when she did it.

'You've fallen in love with a boat called Batavia. If boats are women I ought to be jealous.'

'Suit yourself,' he said cheerfully. 'I could have gone for a trip. I was invited. "Come to Genoa", he said, the fellow that owned it, "I'd like to have you along." '

'And you'd like to go.' She accepted it, in fact she rushed to pick it up. He saw fear in her face. He was about to tell her not to be such a fool when she smiled brilliantly. 'You on a yacht?'

'Why not?'

'My darling, you'd be bored with yacht people.'

'You think I haven't got enough class, is that it?'

'Don't be silly.'

'Things have changed since your day, you know. Since fifty years ago.' Her smile untouched, she put out her hand and with her finger-tips traced the big muscle at the top of his arm. 'There's no class nowadays, there's only money. Anyone can own a yacht – straight, bent or just queer. I'd be OK, I'd be Just Brent. I could have fun.' She hadn't a clue what he was talking about, but he made it sound considerable – as if he was seriously considering it.

Madge was lazy more than she was soft-hearted – 'I didn't like to say', she said. The thing was, she hadn't said it at the right time. 'OK,' he said, 'I'll say it. I don't want to go.' He couldn't see any reason to go anywhere. 'I like it here.' And so did she, left to herself she wouldn't have gone out of the hotel garden.

'It's all arranged for this afternoon.'

'I'll unarrange it.'

They were still in bed and she half sighed, half relaxed, her head turned to him on the pillow. 'Perhaps we should go just this once.'

'Why?'

'Because we're here and it's there.'

'What's there?'

'A perched village.'

'Sounds like a hen.' She let out the other half of her sigh and lay peacefully against him. She had made a stand – all that she was going to make – and now left it up to him. Or down to him, whichever way you looked at it. 'I suppose if we were at Blackpool you'd say we ought to ride the Big Dipper just once, because it was there.' She lifted her head off the pillow, looked down at him, eating him with her eyes. 'Where is this place?'

'Somewhere in the hills. It was nice of them to offer to take us.'

'He puts me in mind of a history teacher we had, O'Goblett his name was. He was always slapping himself. In the middle of telling us about Henry VIII and his wives he'd turn around and slap his own wrists. He must have been having dirty thoughts.'

'Mr Jessel doesn't.'

'Why not? The older they are the more they think.'

'He doesn't slap himself. And he's not so old. Not much older than me.'

She was teasing; they were so close to each other that he heard her tongue and her lips part in a smile. If he spoke about her age he was nearly always angry. She laughed about it, made a thing about being old enough to be his mother. Which she was. He never knew whether to blame himself for that, or her. It was one joke he had to take from her because it was the only way she could talk about the difference in their ages.

He rolled over and kissed her neck, lingered, and eventually slept in it. When he awoke he got up and went for his swim and forgot about the Jessels.

He was lying on his back in the sun when the old fellow came down the beach to say he'd have the car round at three o'clock.

'I trust that will be convenient.'

'What for?'

'I understood we were to make an excursion this afternoon.'

Old Jessel – Mister to me, thought Leslie – stood there like a bank manager in summer, his tie tied, his jacket open on one button, his shady panama resting on the tops of his ears.

Leslie pushed himself up on his elbow. The wet sand dropped off his shoulder blades. 'That'll be OK.'

*

Mrs Jessel told them to call her Connie. She fussed about how they should sit in the car, whether 'the two men' should be in front or would Leslie rather be with his wife. He sat himself in the back seat without further ado.

'We can't keep Mr and Mrs-ing each other, can we?'

Madge just smiled, Mrs Jessel rabbited on about how she had hated her baptismal name as a child but children always did hate their names. Now she thought hers quite suited her.

'I don't hate mine. Leslie Brent's as good a handle as any.'

'It sounds like a film star.'

'That was George,' said Madge.

'I beg your pardon?'

'George Brent, Leslie Howard.'

'Oh. Yes, of course. They were so nice, weren't they? There's nobody like that now.' Leslie saw the old fellow giving her sharpish looks. 'My husband's name is Jim.'

'Formalities over,' Leslie said, but she turned to Madge.

'Madge – is that short for Margaret?'

'And for a magpie.' She leaned against him in the back seat of the car and put her hand on his kneecap. She should have thought of it before, she was the one who had wanted them to come.

When the car started, the engine sounded like a buzz-saw, but then it was kept in low gear. Old Jim Jessel drove down the autoroute steady as a hearse and not much faster. Traffic bunched behind them, hooting. Some people protested after they had got by, holding down their klaxons and shrieking away like express trains.

'Surely it's not necessary to make such a noise!' Mrs Jessel said to her husband.

'They are Continentals.' Approaching a dormobile with a GB plate, he tucked in behind it, constituting a plug in the middle lane. Leslie watched the traffic building up, dodging and jockeying and then breaking out and scorching away on squealing tyres. Presently they left the dormobile trundling and turned off the coast road.

[163]

'I'm glad we hired the car, it's so nice to be able to get about as and when you like. Jim didn't want to bring ours and drive it all the way here.'

If he had, they'd still be coming, thought Leslie. He put his head on Madge's shoulder; he had eaten a big lunch, the car was hot as an oven and he was missing his siesta. Madge said, 'I wanted to get Leslie away from cars for a while.'

'That's not possible, I'm afraid. Internal combustion rules everywhere OK.' Old JJ had made a joke.

'From having to mess about with them,' said Madge. 'Being actively concerned. He is, every day. I wanted him to have a complete break.'

That was what she wanted. You lived, thought Leslie, but you didn't learn much. He had always known that a woman, any woman, wanted to get a man, any man, away from anything he half-way liked doing, and Madge was no exception. The trouble, the root-trouble was that she could have been.

When the road started climbing and there was only scenery to look at he dozed off. He was conscious of the car grinding uphill and being turned back on itself again and again. Then it stalled and JJ said, if not a rude word, a peevish one. Leslie opened an eye. They were on a road above a ravine. A massively shattered viaduct failed to link up two limestone cliffs. Someone with no respect for old drama had thrown mattresses and fridges among the chunks of broken masonry.

'The Germans blew up this bridge,' said Mrs JJ.

JJ corrected her. 'I believe it was the French who did it.'

'So that the Germans shouldn't.'

'So that the Germans shouldn't use it.'

'Well, it's not very pretty. Couldn't we have gone another way?'

JJ, who was having trouble getting the car started on the gradient said, 'I'm afraid not. This is a hilltop village with only one access road.'

'I can't think why they wanted to build up here.'

'It would almost certainly have been a defensive measure.'

Leslie leaned over and pushed in the choke. 'It's flooded. You'll have to wait.'

'On this bend?'

'No choice,' Leslie said cheerfully, 'unless you'd like to coast down backwards.'

Mrs JJ cried, 'Jim – no!' He switched off the engine, rammed home the gear-lever, hauled on the handbrake. 'What happens if someone wants to pass us?' He sat gingerly in his seat, his face stony, in his hair-parting a few beads of sweat. 'Really, it's too bad!' She looked out of the window into the ravine and then at the steering-wheel which her husband was gripping with both hands. 'We've been going to Bournemouth for years – oh I know it sounds fuddy but it's really very nice and the weather's what we're used to and you don't have to fly.'

'We went there for our honeymoon,' said Madge.

'To Bournemouth?' She turned impulsively. 'So did we! Oh how strange! How extraordinary! What a coincidence. Jim, don't you think it's an extraordinary coincidence?'

'It would be better if you sat quite still.'

'Oh good heavens, this stupid car! Of course it was years and years ago, our honeymoon. We stayed at a hotel above one of the chines and they painted the eggs we had for breakfast – the boiled eggs, of course.'

'Painted them?'

'Yes, the shells – with roses and violets, they did it for all the honeymooners.' Mrs JJ blushed, a one-time dimple reviving in her cheek. 'I remember as if it was yesterday.'

'Ours was last year,' said Madge.

'Yours?'

'Our honeymoon.' The dimple vanished. Mrs JJ sat there trying to figure out how old Madge would be, how much older than the man she had married. Leslie could see her doing it, adding up the years. How could she understand? Why should she? What the hell

[165]

business was it of hers? 'I don't remember where we stayed.' Madge said gently, 'We needn't have gone anywhere for all we noticed.'

'Oh,' said Mrs JJ. She snatched up the road map and fanned herself. Well she might, the car was roasting hot. Her old man dived for the ignition, switched on and started the engine. More by luck than judgment they moved off.

The place they were going to was shrouded in mist. They couldn't see it from below.

'I'm afraid visibility will be poor,' said JJ.

'How high is it?'

'Well over a thousand feet. I believe it is the highest occupied village in the area.'

'What's the good if we can't see anything!' cried his wife.

They had to leave the car in a park below the village and go on foot the rest of the way. It was still a climb, and the mist totally enclosed them. They heard and felt the presence of other people but saw them only when they came within arms' reach. Yet when they looked over the remains of what JJ said were ramparts, by some trick of light and the time of day and the position of the sun, they saw through holes in the clouds the enormous shadow of the crag and their own shadows stretching across the valley floor. When Leslie waved both arms over his head the movement was reflected a thousand feet below.

Mrs JJ covered her face. 'I can't look down there.'

'The guidebook is not to be taken as gospel. It is a local publication and prone to exaggeration. However, one may accept what is said about the architecture of the place. Building on this rock could only be extended upwards because of limitations of space. Hence the name, Les Tourelles, The Turrets.'

'Like New York,' said Leslie.

'I beg your pardon?'

'Skyscrapers.' He found that if he kept his eyes on the mist it sank into itself like milk taken off the boil.

Madge shivered. 'I'm cold.'

'Isn't it wretched!' cried Mrs JJ. 'But there are shops, we can go inside.'

The place was crowded: in the one poky street were congregated people in beachtops and bikinis from the hotlands down at the coast, turning mulberry colour and cuddling one another against the cold. Leslie put his arm round Madge, JJ stalked ahead in his linen suit leaving Mrs JJ to cuddle herself.

Of course it had been got up for the benefit of the tourists and was jam-packed with window boxes and Ali Baba jars and pink geraniums. Every signboard was a chunk of olive wood, every lamp was wrought iron, every shop was a boutique. There was a bar with stained-glass windows and stable half-doors, a pizza parlour and an English tea-room. The shops sold spun glass, bracelets, lavender bags, fancy leather, copper egg-timers and marble eggs, nougat, Napoleon brandy, diving-masks, wet suits and fish-guns. But the washing hung across the alleys leading off the main street, the church was in the middle where it had always been, with stone saints and gremlins hanging out all over it and a crack from floor to roof stopped up with bitumen, and old women in the porch, knitting. The mist was everywhere, like a cold sweat.

'Would you care for some tea?' said JJ.

'We could do with a drink.'

'Oh – I thought you didn't,' said Mrs JJ.

'Didn't what?'

'Drink – alcohol, I mean.'

'Why think that?' She looked to Madge as if for help. Madge lifted her brows. Leslie said good-humouredly, 'You've got to have a reason for thinking such a damned silly thing about us.'

Mrs JJ reddened. 'I thought you'd given it up.'

'Turned teetotal?'

'Yes – when Madge was ill.'

'She's never been ill as long as I've known her.'

'Obviously a misunderstanding,' said JJ.

'What sort of illness?'

'Couldn't we just leave it at that?' said JJ.

'I'd like to sort it out for my own satisfaction.'

Madge smiled. 'It won't be for anyone else's.'

Mrs JJ burst out, 'It was when she had a miscarriage. Don't you call that being ill?'

Leslie looked at Madge. Her lips held the smile, her eyes did not. He couldn't see into them or beyond them. When he took her arm he felt it prickly with cold and rubbed it. He was sorry for her then and he dreaded sorrow more than rage. It left them both defenceless.

'Come on, old girl, let's get you a drink.' He drew her into the bar where the stained glass made stained dusk and at least it looked warmer.

He asked for coffee and whisky for Madge and himself. The Jessels joined them. JJ said that as he was driving he would just have coffee. She, with a sideways glance, declared she was chilled to the bone and would take whisky too.

'Is it always cold here?' said Madge.

JJ, helping his wife on to a stool, said the mean temperature was somewhat ungenerous.

Leslie grinned obligingly. You had to be careful not to miss Jimmy O'Goblett's jokes. The poor old sod tried – he couldn't have much to laugh at with a wife like his.

She started to beef about they shouldn't have come, they should have gone along the coast. 'Jim made out it's so lovely in the hills.'

'He couldn't have known there'd be a fog.'

'In point of fact, it's low cloud,' said JJ.

His wife asked him, 'Was it like this where you stayed? When you were here before?'

'Certainly not. For one thing it was nowhere near as high.'

'Big Horn,' she said, and laughed. She had drunk down a whisky and was sipping her coffee. 'That's what it was called, the place he went to years ago.' JJ sat on his stool like a ramrod. Something – the stool or his bones – cracked. 'Big Horn was where he went for his school holiday.'

'The name of the farm was La Bigorne.'

'Low cloud?' Madge looked up from searching in her bag for cigarettes.

'Why didn't you bring a cardigan?' Leslie said to her.

'She would never think she'd need it!' cried Mrs JJ.

JJ said he was sorry if Mrs Brent was suffering discomfort.

Madge smiled. 'I can always go and buy a cardigan.'

She smoked her cigarette and asked for another whisky. Mrs JJ waved to the barman. The barman took no notice. Leslie whistled to him. 'I'd like another one too,' said Mrs JJ. The barman came and JJ ordered in French. He did not look at his wife but she looked at him and made a face. She was feeling the effects of the whisky. Madge had benefited, the warm cream was back in her skin, but Mrs JJ had blown up like a pigeon. Leslie was sorry for her old man, holding his knees on the barstool. He wouldn't have asked for this, it would be all her doing. And as it wasn't turning out right, she was blaming him. But there seemed to be something else she was putting on him, nothing to do with this afternoon, from some time and way back. Couldn't they do better after a hundred years together?

They got up to go and Mrs JJ had Madge to herself while Leslie and JJ were settling the bill. 'Isn't it awful trying to find things to take home? My friend Edith never gets abroad now and I want to take her something, some small memento. But things here aren't all that different from what we can get at home. I think the Common Market had taken away all the surprise.'

By the time Leslie and JJ left the café the women had disappeared. JJ stood looking down the street. Leslie, who was not imaginative, only aggrieved, said 'Roses and violets!'

'I beg your pardon?' said JJ.

'Was that before they were boiled, or after?' He asked in good faith, wanting to know and to commiserate. 'It would have turned me off. All I want on my egg is salt.'

'I'm sorry, I'm not with you.'

But he was, and he was bristling, the short hairs bristled out of his nostrils.

Leslie clapped him on the shoulder. 'Let's go and find the girls.' He made for a shop opposite the bar. People had flocked in on account of the weather but not Madge or Mrs JJ.

Leslie turned and went out in a straight flush of anger. Madge had no rhyme nor reason and, he was sure, no inclination to go off with that woman. She just hadn't bothered herself not to. There were times when what mattered to him didn't even exist to her. Like the expectation that on this damned awful outing she would stay with him. It was the least she could do. He was under no obligation, he hadn't wanted or asked to come, to have to put up with undiluted Jessel. The fact of the matter was that she ought to have wanted to stay with him.

Then he saw her through the doorway of the shop next to the bar. It was maybe five minutes since he had last seen her yet he felt immediate savage relief: savage because he was ready to fight – even to fight her – to keep it. He had had relief the very first time he set eyes on her and he got it now because he lost it now – whenever she removed herself unexpectedly from his sight.

This shop, too, was crowded. He pushed in, meeting an outlandish smell as if someone was burning joss-sticks. They might have been because a Chinaman stood in a corner. He had a pigtail, a string moustache and a skull-cap and a robe down to the floor. The robe had dragons embroidered all over it. He kept his hands tucked in his sleeves, the only part of him that moved was his eyes.

Madge and Mrs JJ were looking at shawls. Madge took one in her hands. She drew it through her fingers, indulging her pleasure at the feel of the silk, reserving a smile at herself.

The shop sold high-class junk, it was a snob trap for tourists. They paid through the nose for stuff that was no use and not much ornament, which they could get at home for half the price and wouldn't miss if they didn't – just to be able to say it came from a place on a pinnacle of rock in the south of France. A man in a T-shirt with a picture of Big Ben on his chest got in Leslie's way. Leslie elbowed him and the man said 'Pardon, monsieur.' Leslie waved and pushed on. Next thing he saw was Mrs JJ taking a shawl and draping it over Madge's shoulders. The shawl was the colour of the clear heat that takes all day to build up at the heart of a fire. Madge held it to her with a half-dreaming, half-mocking expression.

'It suits you.' Mrs JJ, seeing Leslie, cried, 'Doesn't it look lovely?'

Madge turned, holding up her arms so that the silk hung down like wings. 'Does it?'

'Yes.'

'Lovely? Really? Would you say that?' She was smiling at him and at herself, just the two of them.

He said, 'Buy it if you want to.'

'I don't want to.' She turned to Mrs JJ. 'I can't wear shawls, they slide off me. My shoulders are too sloping or too slippery or something.'

'It's sure to be terribly expensive.'

'Wouldn't you like it?' Madge offered the shawl to Mrs JJ.

'Oh no, it wouldn't suit me.'

'I don't see why not.'

'Prices here are bound to be steep,' said JJ, keeping up the tradition.

Madge smiled, Mrs JJ did something else. She lifted the hair off the back of her neck with a gesture which was all Madge's. Leslie couldn't believe his eyes, for it was something Madge did quite unconsciously. He would have known her by it a mile off or in deep disguise. Mrs JJ's hair was short but she put up two fingers and lifted it just like Madge did. 'I've never been able to wear red. Not like you.'

'I don't see why not,' Madge said again. She was bored, Leslie could tell by the way she shrugged off the shawl and dropped it back in its tray. But Mrs JJ took it as a statement of fact. She gave her husband a look of something like triumph.

He didn't seem to register whatever it was she meant him to. He said, 'Perhaps Edith would like some lavender.'

'She can get that at home.'

'Not Provençal lavender.'

'I want to get her something different, a memento of this place.'

JJ raised his eyebrows. 'Can you remind her of somewhere she has not been?'

Leslie caught the Chinaman's eye. It moved so fast it was like catching a tadpole in a jam jar.

'You know what I mean. My friend Edith's a widow,' Mrs JJ said to Madge, 'and rather difficult to please. I suppose it comes of having only herself to think about.'

'French lavender is highly aromatic. It grows wild in the garigue. They dry it in the sun. The perfume is quite overwhelming. I remember –' JJ, stopping himself, had obviously thought better of something – 'someone I knew took the trouble to dry it and put it in bags. I was given some to take home to my mother.'

'I can imagine Edith's face if I took her a bag of lavender.'

'What about this?' Leslie picked up a small ivory figure and held it out on his palm. He wasn't proposing it for Mrs JJ's friend, he thought it might appeal to Madge.

Mrs JJ exclaimed 'Oh how sweet! It's a baby or something.'

'A baby?' Madge took the thing, bent her head to look at it.

Leslie grinned. 'Or something.'

It did look like a baby, a fat, naked creature in a basket with its fist in its mouth. Leslie had seen the sort of thing before: carved out of bone, dirty yellow in colour and the size of his thumb nail. At first sight it looked pretty and harmless: at second it was neither. What this actually was was a bald ugly old man, wearing only a loincloth and biting the head off a dog.

[172]

Mrs JJ was the first to turn away. 'If that's Provençal I'll wait till we get to the airport and buy Edith some duty-free perfume. But not lavender-water. She has very sophisticated tastes.'

'It is oriental,' said JJ. 'I believe these carvings are rather sought after.'

'Made in Hong Kong,' said Leslie.

'It's quite repulsive!'

'It's not a baby,' said Madge.

Leslie laughed. 'Not the kind you'd want in your lap.'

'It's an old man –' She gazed at him, dismayed as if she'd given birth to the thing.

'They are almost invariably grotesque or comic, intended to be worn as ornaments by mandarins. Cartoons in ivory one might call them.'

Leslie went to Madge and put his arms round her. He kissed her long and deep, in front of them all, and she responded, as much in need as he was. They drew apart to find the Jessels in a small panic. She had gone beetroot-red and was slapping down her skirt, trying to look uninvolved.

'I'll go and see if the mist has cleared.' That was Jimmy O'Goblett, slapping his wrist. His wife scuttled out after him.

Leslie took the ivory from Madge and put it back in the show-case. 'We aren't going to wait for the mist.'

But when he had pushed his way through the shop the Jessels were outside. JJ said would they like to go back to the car.

'You bet.'

Leslie turned to watch Madge emerge from the shop. She eased herself through the press of people, her shoulders and thighs accommodating, with a gentleness which was almost voluptuous. If it was, he knew who it was meant for. He went to her, took her arm and locked it under his. They walked together down the hill. The mist was opening up. There were still some fingerable patches, but it was rolling around like steam in a laundry. People came out, the street was filling.

'Let's go back to the hotel.'

She rested her head against his shoulder. 'What about the Jessels?'

'They can do what they like.'

'Suppose they don't want to go back?'

'We'll get a bus.'

'From here?'

As they left the houses behind them a ball of mist came up from the ramparts and spent itself over them, cold as charity. Madge shuddered. Leslie looked round for the Jessels. They were a few paces away. Immediately behind himself and Madge was the China-man. Seeing him there gave Leslie quite a turn. They all, Madge and himself, the Chinaman and the Jessels, stopped in the middle of the car park. The Chinaman rose up tall as a chimney and yellow as a guinea.

'What the hell,' said Leslie.

The Chinaman bowed. 'Mesdames, Messieurs.'

'What do you want?'

'I regret, I must ask for the return of my property.'

'Property? What property?'

He lifted his linked arms, hidden in their long sleeves, in a gesture towards Madge.

Leslie made a mistake then. Between confusion and the rising of his temper and the sinking of something else, he thought the fellow was two lingos short – French and English. He signed to him to get going. 'Savvy?' The Chinaman nodded. 'Do it or you'll savvy my boot.'

'I will gladly go when the lady restores to me the netsuke which she carried away from my shop.'

'The what?'

'I am sorry. The item is valuable, I cannot afford to lose it.'

'I don't give a damn what you can afford!'

'I think he means the ivory carving we were looking at,' said Jessel.

'That? I'd call that a good loss. We put it back where it came from, old sport, and glad to see the last of it.'

The man inclined his head as if acknowledging a compliment. 'The lady, however, laid another hand on it.'

'Which lady?' said JJ.

The Chinaman bowed to Madge.

Leslie looked at the dragons on the man's robe. They were gold, gold thread worked on a green background. He had to admit the design was beautiful. It was hateful too, gold and green were the colours of his hate. He let himself think of ripping it up, feel the cloth giving, hear the sound of it tearing. His palms sweated. He said, 'Give it back.'

Madge looked at him, then at the Jessels. 'I can't.'

'Give it back!'

'I have nothing to give.'

'Heavens!' Mrs JJ rounded on Leslie. 'You really can't think –'

He snatched Madge's handbag and held it out to the Chinaman. 'OK. Look.' The man bowed again, keeping his hands in his sleeves. 'Go on! Look for yourself.'

'You can't!' cried Mrs JJ. 'You can't let him go through her bag!'

Leslie said to Madge, 'It's OK with you, you've nothing to hide.' She wasn't trying to hide anything from him. She couldn't. He could see right through to her secret mess – of fear, deceit and sheer bloody-mindedness. He had seen it often enough to know what was in it. He threw the bag at the Chinaman's feet. 'Find your property.'

'I'll find it – I'll look,' said Mrs JJ.

'The Chink wouldn't trust you and neither would I.'

JJ said sharply, 'What do you mean by that?'

'She'd cover up.'

'Cover up?'

'To protect my wife, and protecting is the last thing she needs.'

Mrs JJ went to pick up the bag but JJ stopped her. 'You're

assuming there is something to cover up?' he said to Leslie, 'although your wife has assured you there is not?'

'You going to look in that bag?' Leslie said to the Chinaman. 'Because no one else is.'

The man, with a practised and unfeminine gesture, gathered up the skirt of his robe, then stooped and picked up the handbag. He looked at Madge. There was no expression on his face. Nor on hers. If he was asking permission, he didn't get it. She waited, without acceptance or meekness.

They watched him open the bag. He inserted his long fingers distastefully, felt about inside.

Madge turned her head away. Mrs JJ clucked like a hen in a sack and people coming to the car park halted at sight of the Chinaman. There wasn't much else to look at, so they looked and hung about looking, at him in his skull-cap, his dragon-embroidered robe and bootlace moustache. Perhaps they thought he was some sort of show put on for the tourists.

He snapped the bag shut with the same sound Leslie had heard Madge close it many a time and held it out.

'You see?' cried Mrs JJ. 'It was nonsense. A pack of lies!'

'Satisfied?' said Leslie.

Madge did not take the bag. The Chinaman stood with it suspended by the handle from his wrist and looking at her left breast where there was a pocket in her blouse, a thin silk blouse that clung in the right places and fell in soft folds where it didn't. There was something in the pocket. Leslie gave himself a second's right of refusal to admit what it was. In the next he had whipped it out and there was no need to look twice. He held it on his palm as he had done in the shop so that they could all see the ugly ivory man. 'Is this yours?'

'Madame, perhaps, meant to buy it.'

'Of course she did!' cried Mrs JJ.

'No she didn't,' said Leslie.

'Perhaps she meant Monsieur to pay for it.'

'No she didn't.'

'Heavens, there must have been *some* misunderstanding!'

'I'll pay for it now,' said Madge.

Leslie tossed the thing up and caught it. 'How much?'

'Eight thousand francs, monsieur.'

'What!'

'It's only about eighty pounds –' She would have taken her bag, but Leslie whipped it off the Chinaman's wrist and thrust it under his own arm.

'The thing's not worth eighty pence.'

'Leslie, please.'

'It is a valuable piece,' said the Chinaman. 'Veritable ivory of the eighteenth century, carved by Kagetoshi and signed by him.'

'I don't care if it's signed by Winston Churchill, we don't want it.' Leslie threw it at the Chinaman who failed to catch it. The netsuke hit the ground, rebounded, then rolled among the grit. There was a pause. On the other side of the car park someone started an engine, but everybody waited – the group immediately round the Chinaman and the people gathered beyond. It was like the moment after a stone hits deep water, before the surface starts to break in a guaranteed pattern and can't be stopped until the last quiver has died away, five minutes hence, or fifty.

The Chinaman walked to where the ivory lay and stooped with dignity to pick it up.

'Leslie, give me my purse.' She had holes where her eyes should be. Well, he hadn't taken her eyes away, she had done that herself and made a guy of him too.

He put the handbag on his chest and locked his arms across it. He started quite quietly saying to her, 'You don't even know you're doing it – now I'm going to let everyone know,' then raised his voice so that all could hear. 'You're a thief and a liar, you're a bloody middle-aged klepto.' Of the Jessels, the Chinaman and people as far as he could reach, he asked, 'Can you think of another way to stop it?'

She turned and ran, she didn't run well, she was too big, panning her feet and beating the air with her hands. Across the car park to the ramparts. The mist was busy on that side of the crag: solid as flannel one minute and the next opening to blue sky and soft white sun. She reached the wall, blundered into it as if she hadn't known it was coming and had thought to go running on into space. She seemed to fold over below the ribs and Mrs JJ cried out in alarm. Hung over the top of the wall she could be sleeping or knocked out or just looking down.

'Oh bring her back!' cried Mrs JJ.

The Chinaman tucked his arms in his sleeves. He asked politely, 'Is she a balanced lady?'

'Balanced?' Leslie looked round at all the faces, the yellow one last. 'What do you think, after what she's done?'

'I think,' JJ said coldly, 'he is referring to her equilibrium, not her state of mind.'

'If you won't fetch her back, I will!' Mrs JJ made as if to run to the ramparts but JJ stopped her.

'Mr Brent will see to his wife.'

Leslie knew they were all against him – the Jessels, the people whose business it certainly wasn't, but who had overheard. A woman said, 'I nearly threw up looking at this place from down below. If I was to look down I guess I'd die.' Even the Chinaman was against him. The Chinaman stared at him from a long way off and it was a lot longer away than China.

Mrs JJ tried to break out of her husband's restraining hold. 'Don't you realise what she must be feeling?' and JJ said sharply to Leslie, 'Mrs Brent is more than a little distressed.'

'Don't you *care?*'

A male voice said, 'The guy's a bastard.'

The Chinaman bowed over his sleeves, murmured, 'I am sorry,' and glided away.

Happy as a sandboy, Leslie went to join Madge at the ramparts. Everyone was one hundred per cent on her side, the side of the lady thief and accredited liar. Madge, his exclusive, beautiful, custom-built Madge, had handled them all – the straight-laced Jessels, the utter strangers, the Hong Kong merchant and her lawful honest-Joe of a husband.

XIV

Connie wanted to know what she could say. What could you say to a woman who had been publicly humiliated by her husband? What could you say to the husband, in the presence of the wife? She was all for leaving them to make their own way back to Antibes.

'There's no bus,' said Jim. 'They would have to hire a taxi.'

'Let them.'

'No. We'll wait.'

'How can I talk to them as if it never happened?'

'You may not have to.' He looked towards the rampart where the Brents stood as one, Leslie's arm crooked round her neck, holding her face to his. 'They may raise the subject themselves.'

'That would be worse.'

'There may be a logical explanation.'

'For what?' Connie had a flicker of hope that something might be redeemable, she saw no need of logic, but she was ready for anything that might explain Madge Brent.

'They seem reconciled.'

'Reconciled!' Yes, she thought, they were, and they were making an exhibition of themselves. Madge Brent had taken and was holding his face in her hands as if it was the most cherished prize. 'I just don't understand her. What logical explanation can there be for the way he behaved?'

'No doubt it seems logical to them.'

'I know you don't care, it doesn't matter to you.' She couldn't call it selfishness because he made all the thoughtful motions towards her, there was thought behind them. Yet all the little things she could depend on him for had not added up to anything of substance or help. 'I've got to understand – I've got to try!'

'I think they're coming.'

Watching them approach she saw the nature and extent of what they had together. They made it obvious, walking hip to hip, enjoying the motions of each other's bodies. His sank into and was expended on hers, Madge Brent's shamelessly and ardently shaped itself to his. He called cheerfully to the Jessels, 'Let's get out of here and find some place with a bit of life.'

'Life?'

'It's not exactly a fun place.' The Brents smiled at each other. Their warmth projected off their skins like sunburn.

In the same way Jim was radiating coldness even through his hat, that awful panama with the pimple upstanding in the centre of the crown – like some sort of final moral judgment, Connie thought wretchedly.

'Whaddya call this?' said Leslie. 'A perched village?'

'It is an apt description.'

'With its craw open for the tourists.'

As they drove out of the car-park Connie gazed blankly through the windscreen, so aware of the Brents at her back that she was unaware of anything in front. She saw in the driving-mirror that Leslie was starting, with purpose and appetite, to devour his wife from the base of her throat to her chin.

'Les Tourelles was first settled by primitive tribes who took advantage of its natural defensive position.' She thought that Jim must have seen it too and was taking his own way out. 'In the course of time it suffered invasion by the Huns, Visigoths, Francs, Lombards and Saracens. It was almost certainly used as an observation post by Roman troops. They built the vallum – the rampart wall, the remains of which now enclose one side of the car-park.'

There was an uneasy pause. Connie found it uneasy because she remembered only too vividly how Madge Brent had hung like a rag doll over that same wall. Jim, remembering or not, cleared his throat and ploughed on. 'It was besieged, decimated by plague and fought over during the wars of religion. Nor did it escape occupation during the war between England and Austria in the eighteenth century, and it was the scene of internecine fighting during the Revolution. I think one can say that Les Tourelles has seen life. In all its aspects.'

'Shame,' Leslie said cosily. 'It deserves something better.'

'I beg your pardon?'

'Better than us poking around and knocking off the junk.'

Connie twisted in her seat to face him. 'Us?'

'Us tourists.' Leslie grinned and she felt herself put in a corner where she didn't belong and couldn't get out of. Jim, concentrating on driving, managed to be separate, from her as well as from the Brents. On her head be it, be it all. She had asked for it. She had asked because of him, because it wasn't true that what you never had you never missed. At this late and pretty well hopeless stage she felt she was missing out on all sorts of alarms and excursions which she might not have been able to handle but should have had the chance to try.

'Is there anywhere you – or Mrs Brent,' said Jim, making a fine distinction, 'would like to go?'

Leslie's head sank into the curve between his wife's chin and breastbone, into its own sized-up socket. If Madge Brent said anything, it was lost in the noise of his yawn.

Jim negotiated the descent. Another car coming down behind them took a chance and roared past, shooting off loose stones at the edge of the abyss. Jim went on down, knuckles white on the wheel, making the car pause and sniff its way round every loop in the road.

XV

Jessel could not positively identify the circus as the one which had frisked with him on the motorway. Connie said it must be the same.

'Not necessarily. There could be several such outfits in the area.'

'Then why have we come to it?'

'Certainly not because I wish to renew acquaintance.'

'Would you recognise the animals? Surely you'd know the lions again!'

Brent, of course, was the reason for their stopping to look at the circus. He had clamoured like a spoiled child and when his wife, who could refuse him nothing, added her pleas, he had switched to adult belligerence. 'Hell, you asked where we wanted to go,' so that Jessel would have been obliged to consent out of common courtesy. At the same time he sensed a threat localised in the back seat of the car but capable of erupting and involving them all. It needed no percipience to appreciate that this man's violence centred on his wife. She, poor woman, rightly and – given the unfortunate circumstances – sometimes wrongly, was the *primum mobile*. To avoid another demonstration like the one at Les Tourelles, Jessel had turned off the road and parked near the motley collection of caravans, lorries, stalls and big-top tent pitched on a dried-up football field. The circus women had slung string between the goal-posts and hung up their washing.

The show, such as it was, looked like doing good business. People were seeking diversion and were prepared to have it thrust upon them without wish or chance of parrying. They were ready to promote it. There was a general air of bravado about the crudity of their expectations.

'Where did the Brents go?' Connie shrugged. He was sorry for her for she, too, had had expectations – of a better sort. A number of young people dressed, or undressed, for the beach, linked arms and broke into the crowd, singing and cheering. Jessel pulled Connie out of their way. 'I have never cared for this sort of thing.'

'They're enjoying themselves.'

'People come here to be taken out of themselves, to lose their identities and their judgment.'

'For heaven's sake!'

'I think it is not too harsh a criticism, considering the nature of the entertainment offered. Performers are required to risk their lives and limbs and wild animals prodded and whipped up to execute unnatural tricks.'

'Perhaps they've gone on the roundabouts.'

'There are no roundabouts.' She had sounded wistful and he wondered what exactly her expectations had been. He had no idea, but since they were not to be fulfilled he felt he should have. His duty, a husband's duty to his wife, was to know without being told.

When she said, 'I think I'll go and have my fortune told,' she seemed to have read his thoughts and taken them a degree further.

'In French?'

'It doesn't matter.'

There, perhaps, his conscience might rest, duty not done, but excused. He hoped that her expectations had in no way concerned himself.

' "Emeraude, Clairvoyante Extraordinaire". That's plain enough,' she said, reading from a board on the side of what looked like a dilapidated Portakabin. 'What does the rest mean?'

' "Diseuse de bonne aventure, conseillère et connaisseuse d'avenir".' He smiled wryly. 'I think it means she can tell your fortune.'

'It's only for a giggle. Will you wait?'

'Of course.'

He watched her approach the rather unsavoury little hut and

knock. The door opened on a flash of green – 'Emeraude', no doubt – and Connie went inside.

He hoped she would find occasion for laughter, if nothing else. Strictly speaking, there should be nothing else. The counsel and forebodings of an itinerant stranger should merely amuse. He feared they would do more. Connie was in a peculiar frame of mind – unframed he might call it. She lacked her usual reservations even, perhaps particularly, as regards themselves. He blamed himself for that. It had been a mistake, a total disaster, to tell her about Mrs Klein. The ghost remained, its essentially private potency gone, as he had wished. What he had not wished, nor foreseen, was that it would be updated and demeaned to make mischief between them. He felt it as a current and continuing disruption. So, he was sure, did Connie, though she would not realise from whence it came. For her day-to-day purposes she had always been quite capable. Having reached a judgment early in their married life she had kept to it and he had been acquiescent, if not content. What she was now seeking was immaterial, it was the fact of her seeking that worried him. He turned his back on the fortune-teller's booth. The potentials were mercifully, and maliciously, hidden from them both.

A running fight was going on between two middle-aged men wearing T-shirts with Union Jacks stitched between their nipples. Women of a certain sort, manifestly not their wives or daughters, were egging them on. One of the women threw back her head and crowed like a cock. Jessel had a detailed glimpse of her throat swelling to accommodate her cries and, beyond, a less detailed but unmistakable glimpse of Waldo Klein.

In any event Waldo was not mistakable. It was something, the greater part, to do with the impression he had already made on the beholder, going back in Jessel's case some fifty years. No one else could ring the same series of bells. Jessel heard them through the shrieks of the women and the shouts of the men.

Unsurprised – he seemed to have accepted that it would be a matter of mere time before this happened, he started towards the red shirt Waldo was wearing and which was now the flag he had to follow. He was confused but hopeful enough to beg 'Excusez-moi' of the crowing women and brawling men. They, not hearing him nor realising that he was trying to pass, sandwiched him between their Union Jacks. When he had struggled free, receiving some gratuitous buffets in the process, Waldo had disappeared.

He pressed on through the crowd with less than his usual ceremony. His apprehension was no less. He felt the old reluctance to encounter Waldo. His detriment remained assured in spite of, perhaps because of, what he now knew. The fact that Waldo's success had been the concealment of his failure was in itself a last irrefutable word.

On one side of the field was a collection of motor caravans and cages partly draped with tarpaulins to give some refuge to the creatures inside. One of the beasts was shouldering to and fro behind bars and Jessel's stomach turned with another, wholly corporal dread.

A boy of about ten or twelve was sitting on the steps of a van playing with a cup and ball. He threw up the ball and caught it with unfailing regularity while Jessel looked about for Waldo. These vans were obviously the living quarters of the circus people, the field beyond was fenced with ugly looking stakes. Jessel was convinced that Waldo had come this way. He said to the boy, 'Have you seen Mr Klein?'

'Pardon?'

Damned French, thought Jessel. He realised that he had spoken out of the single-mindedness which Waldo generated in him. 'Avez-vous vu un homme dans une chemise rouge?'

'Un Communiste?'

'Non, quelqu'un qui porte une chemise rouge.'

'Pourquoi?'

'I don't know – je ne sais pas – it happens to be what he's wearing.' With Daisy's sewing on it? 'Je crois qu'il passe par ici et je veux parler avec lui.'

'Bien sûr.' The child had not interrupted his game. The click of the ball falling into the cup was as regular as the ticking of a big clock.

'Il est mon ami –'

'Vraiment.'

'S'il vous plaît –' Jessel, struggling, thought he sounded as if he were asking for the salt – 'c'est longtempts que je l'ai vu. Il avait disparu.'

The child caught the ball and put his hand over the cup. 'I am trying to break my record. It is three million.'

'Three million?'

'Trois milles prises.'

'He came this way, he must have passed you.'

'That man in the red shirt is not Mr Klein.'

'So you did see him. Where did he go?'

'That man is a driver.'

'A driver?'

'He drives the truck.'

'I see.' What Jessel saw was the circus on the autoroute, the big truck skittishly swerving, taunting, ribbing him to death. Waldo at the wheel of that truck had seen and recognised him and chosen to play cat and mouse, lion and mouse, ape and mouse. He excelled at the impromptu and although there was never any knowing what he would do, when he had done it the pertinency was painfully obvious. Of that much Jessel could be sure. Waldo's games had kept up with the times, but grown man, old man as he was, Jessel experienced the same bitter sense of isolation as at their very first encounter, fifty years ago, when Waldo lobbed a ball at him and had not waited to see him drop it. 'How long has this driver been with the circus?'

'I am away at school, people come and go. My father employs many people.'

'Your father owns the circus?'

'He is the directeur.'

'What does this man call himself?'

The boy frowned. 'He goes to put on his costume.'

'What costume?'

'He drives, also he is a performer. An artiste.'

'Indeed?'

The boy said huffily, 'It requires great power – not strength, that he has also, but here –' he touched his forehead and chest – 'and here, to do as he does.'

'What does he do?'

'He is the derrière – you say the bum – of the elephant.'

'What?'

'There must be an elephant très sagace for the clowns' act. Our elephant is stupid, a stupid beast. So we have two men in the elephant skin. Now, the bum is important, the bum performs the most, sad but comique. It is the super-bum.' He looked sharply at Jessel. 'You understand?'

'I'm afraid I don't.'

'It is necessary to make people laugh. Sit on your hat and they will laugh. Tread into a pail of whitewash and they will laugh. They like to laugh at misfortune.'

'That's true. And this man is prepared to suffer misfortune for their amusement?'

'He is a kind man.' The child threw up his ball and caught it in the cup with a final click. 'Also, he is English.'

'Ah. What is his name?'

'Crow.'

'You mean Crau.'

'He calls himself James Crow. Crow as in "beau". The vowel is not bent, you understand, it is round.'

'I understand.'

'You wish I should bring him to you?'

'No.'

'He is not your friend? The friend you search?'

'No,' said Jessel. 'Thank you.'

The boy stood and made him a little bow. Jessel raised his hand in acknowledgment but the gesture fell short of a wave and looked ridiculously like a papal blessing. The child resumed his game and the precise click of the ball and cup followed Jessel as he walked away. He had a vision of the bead curtain falling into place.

XVI

When Connie came out of the fortune-teller's booth Jim was waiting bare-headed in the sun.

'Where's your hat?'

He put his hand to his head and she realised that he hadn't known that the hat was gone. 'I must have lost it.'

'How could you lose it!'

'Things became rather rough.'

She said, alarmed, 'Not Leslie Brent?'

'No, just people enjoying themselves.'

'What happened?'

'A crowd came by after you left. They were in irresponsible mood and there was some horseplay. My hat must have been knocked off.'

'Have you looked for it?'

'No.'

Her surprise deepened to concern. It was so unlike him, more unlike than any show of violence would have been. But she could see nothing unusual about him, except that there was not enough blood in his eye-sockets. 'It isn't good for you to stand around in the sun. Your hat can't have got far, we must try to find it.'

'I hardly think it will be wearable.' She thought he could be right. At her feet were broken cartons and burst balloons.

They moved away together. She, at least, was looking for his hat when he said, 'Did you hear anything to your advantage from the fortune-teller?'

'Not really.'

'I'm sure she did her best to give you a favourable impression.'

'She spoke English. She'd been to school in Cheltenham. I asked if she went to the ladies' college and she said "Ladyship was not my destiny". Look – isn't that it?'

He stood gazing down at the battered object which might or might not have been a straw hat. The sun found his skull under his thinning hair and sparked off it as if it was a mirror. Connie said, 'Even the pimple's gone.'

'The what?'

'The pimple on top. That woman wasn't the real Emeraude, whoever *she* might be. She was standing in for her and I don't think she knew much about telling fortunes.'

Jim touched the thing with his toe. 'It isn't mine.'

Connie was suddenly struck with the paltriness of the situation. What they were doing was utterly trivial. Asked to account for how they had spent these moments they would be hard put to find words. He wasn't looking for his hat and she didn't believe the mumbo-jumbo she had paid ten francs to be told by someone who didn't know her from Adam. Or Eve.

'No doubt she told you you would shortly be going on a journey across the water.'

When was the last time they did something that really mattered? One hour, two hours ago – that hadn't been their doing. They had been done by. For all she knew, his embarrassment and shock was as deep as hers. 'She said I'd never be rich, but I'd always have enough.'

'A fairly safe assumption.'

'It depends what you mean by enough.' He gazed at her blankly. 'Would you have behaved like Leslie Brent if it was I who had stolen that thing – if it looked as if I had?' Of course she knew what he would do, she wasn't asking to be told. 'Would you show me up in front of everyone?'

'It is a hypothetical question.'

What she wanted to hear was not the answer, but the way it was given. 'I might steal because I was ill or upset or unhappy. It could come over me any time. What would you do if I was caught?'

'I can't envisage the situation.'

'Try.'

He said patiently, 'What I would or would not do will scarcely help you to understand the Brents.'

'It might help me to bear them.' Hearing herself say that was as much of a surprise as it must have been to him.

He coloured slightly, with embarrassment or warmth, she could not tell which. 'I might say that you believed I was paying and that being in a hurry I had omitted to do so. It would be a pardonable lie.'

She saw that she wasn't going to get any more. It was all he was capable of, but it was his all and was offered and who was she – apart from being his wife, which she had better disregard – to complain if his all was less than someone else's?

He took her arm. 'Do you know, I think I'd like to stay and see the show. What do you say?'